T0068034

The Price He Paid

The Price He Paid

SEAN MADDOX

authorHOUSE®

AuthorHouse™
1663 Liberty Drive
Bloomington, IN 47403
www.authorhouse.com
Phone: 1-800-839-8640

Published by AuthorHouse   07/10/2015

ISBN: 978-1-4685-4008-6 (sc)
ISBN: 978-1-4685-4007-9 (e)

Library of Congress Control Number: 2012900198

Print information available on the last page.

CONTENTS

PREFIX

Jesus paid the price for our sins. Jesus died on the cross for our sins. Jesus blood was shed on the cross for our sins. This is the price Jesus paid for you.

When we remember Jesus we remember the price he paid for us. We remember the great sacrifice that was made for us. We remember bloodshed on the cross for our sins. We remember the sacrifice of ones life for our sins so that we might be set free. Free from the world. Free from starvation. Free from sins. Free from tribulation. And free from the adversary.

When I think of the church I think of a holy sanctuary of God. I think of a holy temple of God, a holy church, a holy ministry, a place to worship, a place to be set free, a place to call my own, a place to minister to, a place to love, a place to cherish, and a place to admire.

The holy church of God is a sanctuary. It's a holy temple, a place to worship, a place to be made set free, a place to heal, a place to repent and a place to be made whole. Free from burden, free from strive, free from battles, and free from storms.

No matter what your story might be God has plan for your life and it starts with both Jesus and God setting you free!

I think about the people of the church congregation and the great sacrifice one has made for the body of Christ. The sacrifice one has made to be set free. To be made holy. To be defined as a member of the church of Christ.

I think about the many ministry works of the Lord that take place in the body of Christ and how Jesus has paid the price so that we might be made more holy to the body of Christ.

I think about my ministry and the ministry work that God has blessed me with. I think about the books that I write. The gift that I have. The choices that I have made. The decisions that I have made and how much God loves me. How much God has sent his one and only son Jesus to die on the cross for our sins.

Nothing in the world brings me greater joy than to complete the missionary work that God has set before me.

I think about past biblical characters that have went before the Lord in sacrifice to complete a mission in Christ for the price that Jesus has paid for them.

I pray to inspire readers from all walks of life to find it in their heart to read more. To read issues of life that is relevant to you. To read issues of life that is interesting to you. To read issues of life that is real.

This book "The Price He Paid" has really touched my life, touched my heart, touched my ministry and ultimately changed my focus, future, and life.

The book "The Price He Paid" is jammed packed with titles, chapters, scriptures, hope, and inspiration for all walks of life to enjoy!

God has really blessed me with a gift to write books in which I feel in my heart I am completing a mission for Christ.

I pray that along the way and along my journey you to find it in your heart the reason why God created you so that you to might complete your mission for Christ. Each and everyday that I live I put my faith and trust in both Jesus and God. I trust that God will fight my battles for me. I pray that God will fight my storms for me. I pray that God will fight my trials and tribulation for me. I thank him for it everyday.

God has blessed me with a tremendous opportunity to witness and fellowship with Christ like believer from all walks of life. God has been there for me every step of the way and thank him for his goodness and mercy.

There is such a therapeutic feeling from being apart of the body of Christ. There is such a therapeutic feeling to completing missionary work for the Lord. God has made it known as he let it be known that his works are the greatest works in the history of the world.

The bible is the greatest piece of literature ever written. It's scriptures, characters, titles, books, chapters, pages, and words are tremendous and sustain the test of time going down as the greatest works in the history of the world.

It brings me great joy to present to you a piece of literature that is very close to my heart. It brings me even greater joy to know that we save lives into the kingdom of God.

There will be a day where we all rejoice in the tremendous goodness and mercy of the Lord Jesus Christ. The day will be soon! Jesus is coming back for you. Jesus is coming back! In the name of your son Jesus Christ Amen.

CHAPTER 1

Finding Who You Are

Many don't believe it but God put you on this earth for a reason. Don't waste your talent. You have to find what moves you. You have to find the hustler spirit that comes from within. We all have the hustler's spirit; don't let anyone tell you different. You have plenty to offer the world. Let your soul bleed. When I say let your soul bleed we are discussing the importance of putting your life on the line sacrificing all that you can to make your dreams come true. God has called you out before the foundation of the world to create a plan for your life that he will complete through you. You cannot pay attention to haters. Haters are jealous because they have not found what it is that makes them complete. They feel left out or don't feel complete because they have not found themselves yet. Once they have found themselves and have become at peace with themselves then they will become complete with life.

Many Christians struggle with finding that they are as a person. Christians listen to the voices in their head about what others are saying about them and their circumstances. As a Christian believer you have to find what it is that you love. This helps in the process of finding who you are as a person.

As a Christian believer when you are yourself you are not focused on being something that your not. You allow yourself to find yourself. You must learn to get a feel for yourself. God is looking to build a lasting relationship with you.

You cannot worry about what others may think or say about you. What another person says about you in a negative manner does not define your inner self in the person you are, the person you will be, the person you plan to be, the person you are growing to be, and the person that you will grow to become. There are thousands of self help Christian books printed to help all Christians with there walk with the Lord. Why is this book any different the any other Christian book throughout the world? This book is written for you the late bloomer in life. The person who was told that you would never amount to anything in life. The person who thought they would not make it in life. The person who thought it was to late to make something of themselves along with the people around them. There are millions of individuals who struggle with who they are as a person because they don't feel good about themselves. On the inside they feel horrible. The adversary is eating at their heart, mind, body, soul, and spirit throughout life. The have not come to the conclusion that God truly does love them and God has a plan for their life.

This is not some sort of a hustle or a game. Life is real and should not be treated as a game. Maybe you are tired of meeting the wrong people. Maybe you are tired of not meeting the people that are in your league or class. You may feel that everyone person that comes along your path was not truly meant for you. You have something special to offer the world. You have something to share with the kingdom of God that God is working through the light that shines bright through you.

Many people cannot understand the bright light that shines through you because they have been trapped in the dark for so long. They do not understand the Christian ways that you have within yourself. They have conformed themselves to the ways of the world and have allowed the world to control and manipulate them. You cannot allow yourself to set back and surround yourself with these people. You have to start surrounding yourself with positive people. Once you start feeling good about yourself, you will start feeling good about the things that God is doing in your life. You should feel good about the way God created you. God created you unique for a reason. God did not create you to be taken advantage of. God created you in the likeness in him. This means you walk, act, and talk like Christ. You carry yourself in a way that leads by example. God created you to be an ambassador for Christ. We know that this book was written to help you grow closer to God. Finding who you are is part of that process. There are people around you who love you for the person that you are. They appreciate the person you are and the person that you have grown to be. These are your Christian brothers and sisters. These are the people that will have eternal life with you in heaven. These are the people you should surround yourself with.

You have been equipped with talents that you should use to your advantage. We all are gifted in talented in numerous ways. God created us this way on purpose so that we may share the gifts, talents, and traits that we have. God loves you more than you can imagine. It may not seem that way to you in the past because of all the struggles and adversities that you have had to overcome, but God loves you. Do not worry about if you are not good enough. Sure you are good enough. You have what it takes to make it. God has equipped you with all that you need in life.

If you have struggled in the past about finding yourself as a person its because you have failed to build a lasting relationship with God. When you build a relationship with God all things come into place. The universe begins to line up in your favor and God begins to reveal the plans that he has in store for you.

You may have been left in the dark or isolated, but God has something great in store for you. Everyone needs that extra reminder again and again to keep them on track for the plans that God has in store for them. Well you might be thinking well how do I find the plans that God has in store for me? Through building a relationship with God and communicating with God. We communicate with God through prayer and speaking in tongues. Speaking is tongues are perfect prayer to God. It's access to a gateway of communication. Many of the problems you are facing can be turned over to God through prayer. Simply go to God in prayer. Tell him what it is that you need.

When you are praying always start or end your prayer "in the name of your son Jesus Christ." It's important to always pray through Jesus. We you pray through Jesus you are respecting and honoring God that Jesus was sent in this world to die for your sins. Its part of the gifts and talents that God has blessed you with. God loves you more than you can imagine which is the reason why you are reminded of it. You begin to build a relationship with God as you continue to go to God in prayer. You lift up your problems to the Lord.

You cannot live your life with all the burden and strife and expect to get positive results throughout life. The burden and strife must be lifted from you. Hand over your problems to God. Go to God in prayer. This is all a part of the process of finding yourself. It's what God wants you to do. Never be afraid to ask God for your needs and wants. You cannot get caught up in the things of this world. You have to allow yourself free time to spend with the Lord at all times. Remember to always put God first throughout your life and all things will fall into place. God has something special planned for your life, which is the reason you are reminded of it. To often time we are busy with our own agendas that we don't make time for God the maker of heaven and earth. Take time to get your life together. You should care about your life enough to pull together. You should believe in yourself enough to make something out of your life. Remember to keep it simple. You never want to complicate things attracted distractions to the plans that God has in store for you. We know that the adversary comes to kill, steal, and destroy.

John 10:10 (King James Version)
10The thief cometh not, but for to steal, and to kill, and to destroy: I am come that they might have life, and that they might have it more abundantly.

Stay focused on the plans that God has in store for you. Continue to stay in prayer asking God for things that you need. Nothing is too big for God to handle. Remember our God will not run out of resources, he will not run out of options.

When you are attempting to find yourself you go through changes. You change the person that you are. You change your identity. You hide behind something that your not. All of your problems weigh in to your identity. You carry a heavy burden on your soul that eats away at your heart and corrupts your soul.

You are continually growing as your find yourself and build a relationship with God. God is molding you into the figure that he wants to develop you into. You may be tired of the old person that you once were, that's because God is about to transform you into a new person. A new self. A person that you will be happy with. You are special to God's heart. God would not have created you if he didn't think that you were special. You get rid of the old and take on the new. You make room for new things in your life that God is doing in your life. The new things a part of a new start. There part of a new season. A new opening to a spiritual realm that will allow you to become productive for the many plans that God has in store for you. God has been molding you in the likeness of him since day one. God is ready to magnify his love for you so that all may know of it. You do not have to try to hide God. If you feel you have to hide God or keep him away from your family and friends you are not associating yourself with the right people. It is time for change in your family and friends. You can still love them, but it doesn't mean you have to associate with them. God has something greater in store for you. Follow the plans that God has in store for you and you can't go wrong.

One of the reasons individuals struggle with their identity is they struggle with becoming a hypocrite. They say one thing and mean or do another. They cannot keep up with themselves. They are to busy trying to impress others that they don't make time. They say they live a holy or Christian life, but they are continuing to do those things that do not line up with the plans that God has in store for them. As a Christian believer you cannot become a hypocrite. You have to do those things that go accordingly to the plans that God has in store for you.

You struggle with finding yourself because you simply will not be yourself. You become to caught up with trying to be something your not. To caught up in trying to impress friends who are truly not your friends. When you find who you are, you find the person that God created you to be. You find the person that you have grown to be. The person that has overcome. The person that has gone through a storm, a battle, pit fall, and peaks. You develop a motivation about yourself. You also begin to learn more about yourself that you did not know. You begin to find talents that you are great at. God begins to reveal more to you. Sure it can be stressful at time, but what's a life without pressure. Its part of life and we must accept it. You begin to learn to accept who you are. God is a God of multiplication.

Do not worry about being someone your not. Most people simply go through this stage of life for a short period of time. You grow as you mature. You grow into the person that God has created you to be throughout life. God has created you to become something special. God has created you to be yourself. God wants you to grow, so that he may teach you talents, traits, dreams, goals, and desires. God has a plan for your life and it all starts with you. God is ready to show up and show out in your life. God has great things in store for you. The sooner you build a relationship with God the sooner God will begin to tell you the plans that he has in store for you. You begin to learn what works. God is always showing you new things. Continue to do those things that you know are right in the eyes of God. God has a plan for your life. God has great things in store for your life and it all starts with you. It all starts with building a lasting relationship with God the maker of heaven and earth. God is a good God.

CHAPTER 2

The Calling

The calling is the mission in which you have been chosen to accomplish with the life given to you. We all have a calling in life. A way to live our life. A purpose. A reason in which we exist. This chapter is written to help you find your calling in life. Its part of the reason in which you exist. God gives you the plans that he has for you to carry out. You cannot go through life expecting to live the life that you want to live without first living a life for God. This life requires you to complete the calling in which God has given you.

Your calling in life is the reason in which you exist. Your calling is the assignment in which you will complete. We all have a calling in life. We all have a reason for which we exist. You were not simply created for any reason. There is a reason for which you exist. Examine the gifts, talents, and traits that God has blessed you with. What talents do you hold? What ideas, concepts, and believes are you good at? This is part of the reason in which you exist. This is part of your calling. God needs for you to live your life to the best of your ability. You will live your life to the best of your ability by focusing on the gifts that God has given you. God needs you to focus on your strengths rather than your weaknesses. When you focus on your strengths, you focus on the things that you are good at. The things that comes natural to you. These are gifts that God has blessed you with, because God wants you to use them for your calling. He wants you to use your gifts to help you advance higher in life. We focus on those things that are higher in live because we are all trying to reach that next level. We are all trying to advance our personal living situation for the better. By using your gifts and talents you can make a career out of the gifts, talents, and traits that God has blessed you with. God would not have given you those talents if he didn't feel that you could not make a career out of what it is that your gifted at. God needs for you to use the talents he has given you to advance the kingdom of God. There are too many people throughout the world who are stuck in fields or industries they don't even like. Some people are forced to do things that truly do not love or have a passion for to earn money to provide for them. These are the realities of what the world has come to. Struggle to survive. Life is made on decisions. Life is based on choices. The choices that you make affect your destiny and the direction in which your life is headed for the future. God has given you the free will choice to worship him. God does not force you to worship him. It is all based of the choices that you make in life.

Your calling is part of a greater sacrifice. Its part of the reason in which you risk your life for the ones that you love. You risk your life because you love those ones around you. You love what they do for you. You love how they support you. You love the affect they have on people. Your conscious leads you towards the calling that you have in life. Your calling is the mission in which you will complete with the life that was given to you on the face of the earth. God would not have created you if he did not believe that he would complete a mission in you. God trust you with a mission because he loves you. God has given you the chance to receive eternal life. The eternal life that is given to you is given to you through you accepting Christ as your Lord and savior. All throughout this book "The Price He Paid", we have discussed ways to accept Christ as your Lord and savior in which you will receive eternal life and live in heaven forever. Your calling requires you to sacrifice your life to receive what more God has in store for you. You use the sacrifice of your life as leverage to gain life that becomes eternal, which is done through Jesus who is responsible for giving you eternal life.

The adversary knows that you have a calling in life. This is the reason in which he works so hard to sell your soul in which you become a slave for him eternally in his kingdom. The adversary will do everything in his power to keep you away from the plans that God has in store for you, which is the reason this is repeated throughout this book. Many of you have been facing devils, adversaries, and storms of your own. When you are closest to your calling this is when the adversary will fight you the hardest. The adversary or the devil knows that God has something great in store for you. He fights hard to win your soul over in which he knows has he control of your destiny. We know that the adversary was once an angel named Michael in the kingdom of heaven, but was thrown out of heaven due to the results of his own greed. God takes his hand of favor off of you when he cannot trust you. This is the reason why God has trust you with a mission or calling because he feels that he can trust you. He knows that you will carry out a mission or purpose under the authority of the Lord.

God called you out before the foundation of the world. God knew he would complete a mission in you long before he created you. Many people go through life not answering the call in which God has given them. Many people are afraid of what God might say. Afraid of the mistakes they have made in their past. Many people simply just do not know God or believe in God. I do believe that God gives everyone a chance to complete his or her calling. Will you answer the call? Will you live your life for God and all that God has in store for you? God would not have created you if he did not have purpose for you. Its time for you to start living your life right. You might fall victim to living a sinful life or a life for the adversary in the past, but it does not always have to be that way. There are millions of people throughout the world that change their life for God and become closer to God. People that were crack attics, dope dealers, drug lords, prostitutes, rape suspects, kidnappers and murders that changed their life around. They found God. God grew closer to them. People find God along the way, because they realize they cannot live their life alone. They realize they cannot live a life in the world without God. God is the reason for the existence. God is the reason in which they were created. God says you can do all things through Christ, which strengthened you.

Philippians 4:13 (New King James Version)
13 I can do all things through Christ [a] who strengthens me.

God gives you a calling because he knows that you can handle the mission. He knows that you will live your life with a purpose. There are to many people that are not living their life with a purpose. They are living their life to simply live. Living their life for the world and not God. Many people have not known God. Many people have only opened their eyes to what the world has to offer. The world indeed does have a lot to offer. There are so many choices, avenues, and streets to maximize the results of your personal search for the desires of your heart. So many avenues to explore in this great big world that God have blessed us with. Our deepest fear is that we are adequate beyond human measure. We fear that our mind is so powerful that we cannot execute on the functions of making our thoughts our realities. We are powerful beyond measure. We have the favor of all mighty God. Remember God will not give you anything that you cannot handle. You might want to start of new magazine, book, or explore a singing career. If God has given you the gift to sing by all means use your gifts to the best of your ability. God would not bless you with a gift if he did not want you to answer the calling. Your gift is part of the reason in which you exist. It's your calling. God needs for you to perform your calling to complete a mission through Jesus. God would not give you the gift if he did not think that you could handle it. When you ignore God you ignore the gifts that God has given to you to complete your calling in life. We all have a calling in life. A purpose for which we exist. God gives you your calling because he knows that you will carry out the mission through Christ. He knows that you will fulfill your purpose for which your were created.

When you are afraid to complete your mission you risk holding up the kingdom of God. You hold up the plans that God has in store for the whole kingdom not simply you alone. This is a statement that is close to my heart. God takes unordinary people and uses them in extraordinary ways. That means that God uses common people like you and me to do amazing things. God used David to fight lions and the giant Goliath. God used Noah to build a massive ark to save the world from the flood in the first world. God used Moses to part the red sea. God used Jesus to turn water into wine. God does miracles the same as he did in the bible times we read about. Miracles happen everyday. They are real and they are part of the way that God perform. God works in mysterious ways. God is never late and always on time.

If you are a person that is afraid to answer the calling or afraid to talk to God, let me be the first to tell you that God still loves you. There are no sure answers except from God to reason why bad things happen to good people in life. Do not let that be the reason why you stop loving God. Do not let that separate you from the great things God will do in your life. God is ready to perform miracles in your life. God is ready to thrust you to a new level. God does not want you to stay stuck in the same rut all the time.

Do not let the gifts and talents that God has given you go to waste. God wants you to use those gifts to the best of your ability. Some feel that you only get one shot in life. That you only receive one calling throughout your lifetime. I believe that God is a God of mercy. A God that forgives his children for the mistakes or past sins they have committed. The devil will try to tempt you this is the reason in which you must be strong-minded. The devil preys on those who posses weak minds. Some say only the strong survive which is a statement that remains true in sports, politics, and life. Strong-minded individuals have a better percent chance of accomplishing the dreams, goals, and ambitions they have set for themselves than one of weaker mind. This is the reason in which the adversary fights so hard to control your mind or the way that you are thinking. We must keep a renewed mind. A renewed mind is the transformation of ones eternal thoughts. When you are transformed you are transformed into the renewed spirit of God. A spirit that becomes holy. A spirit that becomes personal to you. It's the spirit in which you carry or posses that will lead you to your destiny. Before you were saved you lived for the world. Before you were saved you did those things of the world only. You did not have the spiritual intelligence to maneuver your way through a corrupted underworld of adversaries that honed in on controlling your mind. God has blessed you with this intelligence to become smart enough to know well from evil. But not only to know good from evil, but also to find yourself as you guide yourself to your true calling in life. You cannot complete your calling in life without first expecting to know God. You must learn to build a relationship with God. When you build a relationship with God you begin to know God on a personal level. You begin to build a bond between you and God in which you form chemistry between the pair. When you form chemistry you form a rapport. You now become close in which you are gelled together as part of a covenant that cannot broken.

Your calling begins with you first accepting Jesus as your Lord and savior. When you accept Jesus as your Lord and savior you form as we just learned a covenant or an incorruptible seed between you and God. This means that this seed cannot be broken. There is nothing that adversary can do to keep you away from the promises that God has in store for you. This is the love that God has in store for you. God loves you more than you can imagine. God sent Jesus to die for you on the cross so that you might have life and have it eternal. This is the reason so many people wear a cross around their neck. This is the reason we take communion at church, to remember what Jesus did for us. To remember that Jesus died for your sins. For this, you should be great full for all that Jesus has done for you. We know that you to can save lives. God rewards those who seek after him. In order to save lives meaning that you are responsible for the destiny in which one has eternal life in the kingdom of heaven you can recite two scriptures in the bible that gives one eternal life in heaven. These two scriptures we know are John 3:16 and Romans 10:9.

John 3:16 (King James Version)
16For God so loved the world that he gave his only begotten Son, that whosoever believeth in him should not perish, but have everlasting life.

Romans 10:9 (King James Version)
9That if thou salt confess with thy mouth the Lord Jesus, and shalt believe in thine heart that God hath raised him from the dead, thou shalt be saved.

God is a good God. Use the power God has given you to complete your calling in life in which you save lives with these two scriptures. Help others people to save more lives so we may all go to heaven. God is good God.

CHAPTER 3

The Late Bloomer

"The Price He Paid", was written for individuals who feel they have had a late start in life. Individuals who feel they have not achieved a level of success that they are looking to achieve. As a Christian believer, God has granted us the power to live our dreams out to fullest throughout the community in which we live.

No matter where you are with your walk with the Lord God has given you the power to accumulate the things that you want most out of life. Everyone has a late start in life. Everyone gets off to a bad start at some point or another. The adversary or the devil comes to kill, steal and to destroy.

John 10:10 (King James Version)
10The thief cometh not, but for to steal, and to kill, and to destroy: I am come that they might have life, and that they might have it more abundantly.

God planned for you to have life and have it more abundantly. God did not plan for you to live in defeat. God planned for you to prosper and be in health.

You may have been let down in the past about past situations that have occurred in your life, but you do not have to settle for less. God has enabled you the power to achieve success, abundance, and to multiply the fruits of the seeds in which you plant.

"The Price He Paid", is the one that has had a late start in life. The person that has failed numerous of times before achieving the success in which one is destined for. We all are destined for something. We are not living simply to live. We live our life with a purpose. We live our lives in the likeness of God the father almighty, maker of heaven and earth. No matter where you are in life, you can achieve the success in which you plan to receive. God has a plan for your life and it all starts with you. It all starts with you making the decision that you are going to live your life for God and no one else. You have the ability to take hold of your life. God is ready to perform miracles in your life that you never thought possible before.

When you begin to find yourself you begin to know God. You begin to know the plans that God has in store for you. You begin to listen to your surroundings, what God is telling you, and what God has in store for you. You do not lean unto your own understanding.

Proverbs 3:5 (King James Version)
5 Trust in the LORD with all thine heart; and lean not unto thine own understanding.

When you lean not unto your own understanding you are trusting God. You trust what God is saying about you. You trust your spirit. You trust your inner self. God allows you to develop an inner self or an inner conscious about yourself you never knew you had. Some of you are just discovering God. You are just discovering the possibilities, outcomes, and variations of what God has to offer and this is perfectly fine.

What is it about God that attracts you to the light? What is it about God that allows you to feel good about yourself? Is it the fact that God is hearing for you? Is it the fact that God loves you? Whatever the reason may be you are growing closer to God. God is building a relationship with you. God is ready to build a lasting relationship with you. God is ready to thrust you to a new level. There are new levels of opportunity all around you. God has something great in store for you.

As a Christian believer you become real with yourself when you begin to know God. You begin to receive a feel for yourself. Whatever you level of success or your walk with God is we all need that extra reminder to keep us on the right track in life.

"The Price He Paid", allows you find yourself. It's important to find yourself. Millions of people are lost. Millions of people are scared of who they are, lost about who they are, and do not know who they are as a person. In this book you will find who you are as true person. You will discover the plans that God has in store for you through finding who you are as a person. Do not let the adversary deceive you. Do not let the adversary tell you different. The adversary will always try to tell you that it's okay to feed into his hands. These are the works of the devil. The devil will always manipulate you into believing the lie of the world.

John 15:19 (King James Version)
19If ye were of the world, the world would love his own: but because ye are not of the world, but I have chosen you out of the world, therefore the world hateth you.

You are not of this world. You have been put in this world temporarily for a mission or a purpose to serve God. As a Christian believer your mission in life is to save lives. You were put on this earth to be fruitful and reproduce in the fruit of the land.

Genesis 1:28 (King James Version)
28And God blessed them, and God said unto them, be fruitful, and multiply, and replenish the earth, and subdue it: and have dominion over the fish of the sea, and over the fowl of the air, and over every living thing that moveth upon the earth.

In the beginning of the bible in the first book Genesis, God instructs us to be fruitful and to multiply. This is part of the plans that God has in store for us. God planned for us to replenish the earth.

"The Price He Paid", in life you are special to God. You are part of an incorruptible seed that cannot be broken. God planned you in the womb that you may be fruit and replenish the earth. It is God that gives us the power to accumulate the necessities that we need from life. You are a child of the highest God. You have been set out apart from the world.

Ephesians 1:4 (King James Version)
4According as he hath chosen us in him before the foundation of the world, that we should be holy and without blame before him in love:

When you are called out before the foundation of the world, you are set apart from the world. You are called for a destiny, a purpose, or a mission. God created you in the likeness of him. God created you so that you may be Christ like. You walk, talk, and act like Christ. You begin to become one with God. One with the spirit. One with the creator of heaven and earth.

All throughout life God is continuing to develop you into the mold, the character, and the person that he wants you to be. You do not get there alone. Everyone does not get there the same way. We all come from different walks of life. Some more respected than others, but we are all children of God nonetheless. God's plans for your life consists of ones that will allow you to take hold of your life. God continues to work on you until he has molded you into the likeness of Christ. Your Christ like mold allows you to develop a character within you that develops your true self. We are all looking for self. God is ready to develop you if you allow him the time to. You do not have to settle for less. God breeds Christians. God breeds a new breed of believers that belong to the body of Christ. Believers that have set out to achieve a level of success that has not been reached yet. A level of success that has not been touched. You reach this level of success through finding God. You do not have shrink back or live in fear anymore. You can live your life in the upbringing of Christ all mighty. You can develop a character within you that allows you to know God. As you grow closer to God, we know that you build a relationship with him. In this book you will discover how to build a relationship with God. You will have the power to make your thoughts a reality.

You learn what is means to be patient. What it means to listen to God. Do not sit back and listen to what the adversary has to say about you. Take control of your life. Choose to do the right things with your life. Make every moment count. Live your life to the fullest having no regrets about the choices that you have made in life. God grants you the power to your success. God gives you life. Life is a gift and should be treated as one. As you continue to grow with Christ, you begin to learn more about yourself. In this book you will know what it means to learn more about yourself as a person. You will find why you aren't receiving blessings. What blessings God has in store for you. Face your downfalls as they come to you. Do not be afraid of failure. Failure comes throughout life because you are not prepared. You are not prepared for what life holds for you. You have the ability to control your destiny.

God has great things in store for you when you believe. You have to learn to build your believe system. Your believe system allows you to believe that all things are possible through Jesus our Lord and savior. God is ready to do great things in your life when you believe. God is ready to perform miracles in your life. You have blessings in store for you right around the corner.

As a Christian believer you do not have to settle for less. Allow yourself time to breathe. Allow yourself time to respond to what the universe is saying about you. Learn how to control your every thought, your every move, and what others are saying about you. Begin to help others grow closer to God as you grow closer to God yourself. Your walk with the Lord is important to you but ultimately important to God. God loves you more than you can imagine. God is ready to perform miracles in your life. God is ready to show up and show out. Get ready for the overflow of abundance that God has in store for you when you believe. God is a good God.

CHAPTER 4

Preparing For The Future

Are you prepared for the future? Are you prepared for Jesus' return? Jesus will return in which you should be prepared to ascend into heaven. God has prepared a place for you to feast at the heavenly banquet. The life given to you on earth simply temporary. You will not remain on earth forever. You will be brought up to heavenly place. God's love for you stretches out further than you can imagine. God's love for you is deeper than you can imagine. It runs deeper than the oceans.

God ask that you prepare for him through knowing him in Christ name. We know God by simply building a relationship with Christ. There are numerous ways to build your relationship with Christ. One way is to go to God in prayer or speaking in tongues. When we pray or speak in tongues you are representing perfect prayer to God. We lift up our inner most thoughts towards the outcomes of our life. We let them be known unto God our situations at hand in which God is prepared to answer your prayers. This is one way you grow closer to God. As you continue to let your prayers be known unto God, you begin to build a relationship with Christ. You learn the plans that God has in store for you. You begin to learn the reasons God has placed certain people in your life. God is seeking to build a relationship with you. God is seeking to know you more. The love that God has for you is sent through his son Jesus Christ, so that you may have life eternal. God planned for you to have everlasting life in the kingdom of heaven. This is why he has sent you on a mission in life to save lives.

We now live in a time in which we should be preparing for our future. Preparing for the return of Jesus. There will be a day in which Jesus returns for his people and we will be sent into the heavens. Are you prepared for this day? Are you living your life for Christ? You may be a person that has not known Christ in the past. You may have grown distant towards Christ. God has been waiting for the day you will return to his love. God has a special plan for your life. Maybe your past has not gone the way that intended. Maybe you have caught some bad breaks, failed, had heartache, or had pain inflicted on your life.

Hebrews 13:5 (King James Version)
5Let your conversation is without covetousness; and be content with such things as ye have: for he hath said, I will never leave thee, nor forsake thee.

This is part of the love that God has for you. God knows that you have messed up in your past. God knows that you have sinned which is the reason why God allows you to come to him in forgiveness. This is the reason why we repent of our sins. We you repent of your sins, you are washing away all of the sins in which you have committed. God does not allow you to repent of your sins to simply abuse the power. The reason in which people's lives have not reached a level of success in the past is because they have failed to plan. Planning allows you to strategically think through your ideas, outcomes, plans, and criteria in which you face at hand, allowing you to carefully think through ideas to orchestrate sound outcomes of ones tasks. God loves individuals who plan. When you don't plan you are setting yourself up for failure. You must be prepared for your future and preparation is the key. When you plan for your future you include the ideas, concepts, and believes written in the word the line up according to the plans of your life. You are not concerned with the ways of the world and how others might live their life. You know that God has plan for your life in which you will complete.

When planning for your future, you must keep a sound mind. A sound mind is a renewed mind. When you renew your mind you allow a transformation of your most internal thoughts to be conformed to the ways of the Holy Spirit. You receive a spiritual intelligence you did not once have before because God wants you to know his ways. Before you were saved you lived your life to the ways of the world. You lived your life to other people's standards. God allowed you to renew your mind receiving spiritual intelligence so that you may know him and know his ways. God wants you to live your life according to his principals. God needs for you to be obedient for the plans that he has in store for you. When you are obedient in Christ, you receive the fruit of the spirit. We know that the fruit of the spirit is part of an incorruptible seed that cannot be broken. It's a seed that cannot be taken away from you. It was given to you before the foundation of the world. Before you were saved you might think back to the times that your life went around in circles. You were living your life without the blessing of being saved. You do not have the spiritual intelligence to learn from your lessons. All you know is the way of the world.

Being prepared for your future requires for you to be disciplined. It requires you to listen to the plans that God has in store for you. You must also listen to the commands that God is telling you. You cannot hear from God when you are too busy living your life to the world's standards or living your life for someone else. This is what happens when the adversary knows that God has something special in store for you. It runs through your veins. This same blood was with the prophets Moses, Noah, and David when they parted the red sea, built an ark, and defeated Goliath. Your blood allows you to do great things on behalf of God for the kingdom of God. Each and everyday we are pressing towards the mark of victory. We are not simply living our lives to just live. We are living our lives for Christ. Each day we lead by example, as we are obedient to Christ for the plans that he has in store for us Christian believers. It is okay if you have been distant from God. Many people are afraid to come back to Jesus. They are afraid of what he might think or what he might say. Know that God loves you the same today, tomorrow, and forever. This is the reason we should never abuse the power of all mighty God.

Philippians 4:6 (King James Version)
6Be careful for nothing; but in every thing by prayer and supplication with thanksgiving let your requests be made known unto God.

When you let your request be made known unto God you lift up your inner prayers, your inner desires, and your inner feelings. These feeling express the love that you have for God. Your feelings, desires, and prayers are part of a testimony of life that is shared with a personal relationship with God. Each and every testimony is part of your destiny in which your will reach. Our testimonies are powerful stories that are shared with Christ like believers to grow closer to one another through learning the different outcomes of a situation. God delivers you through pitfalls, storms, and battles of life that are put in your life to make you stronger. Remember God will not give you more than you can handle. God is there for you every step of the way, which is the reason why we go to God in prayer. We lift up our inner most thoughts that are personal to God, Jesus and you. God delivers you as you draw closer to him and you seek him. A wise man seeks wisdom in which he can maneuver through the darkness of the adversary. Wisdom allows one to grow with God. When you are wise you store the treasures of life the run closet to you. You now discover the answer to life. The answers that you have been seeking.

Many people do not know why we face battles. We face battles to become strong. We face battles to become wise. We face battles to become prepared what God has in store for us next. Its all apart of being prepared for what God has greater in store for us. God wants you to be happy. God does not want you to go around defeat, depressed, and living in misery. The adversary wants those things for you. We talk about the adversary a lot to make known to your conscious that you will be under attack now that you know God. The adversary doesn't want you to make it, but God says differently. This is why we must put our faith in God and not man. Man does not have the last say so. Man cannot move a mountain.

Matthew 17:20 (King James Version)
20And Jesus said unto them, Because of your unbelief: for verily I say unto you, If ye have faith as a grain of mustard seed, ye shall say unto this mountain, Remove hence to yonder place; and it shall remove; and nothing shall be impossible unto you.

God holds the power to move mountains when you have faith the size of mustard seed. This is the power that God has from within for all who love him. Maybe you have been distant from God in the past. Maybe you stopped going to church, stop believing in God or simply feel there is no God. God is here to say that he loves you. God is here to say that he has a plan for your life. God wants you to prosper. He wants you to succeed. God's word is pure. It's the truth and it's filled with fruit. You gain so much insight from reading the bible. Simply read your favorite scriptures from the word of God to learn the plans that God has in store for you. Live your life according to the plans that God has laid out for his believers.

Do not leave room for yourself to fail, by not planning for your future. You do not have to live your life that way everyone else is living there's. DO not make the mistake or fall in the trap of keeping up with the Jones. This phrase is used when others attempt to compete or keep up with ones materialistic personal value to gain what the world has to offer. You see a neighbor by a new car, so you go out and by a new car. Your cousin gets a new home, now you want a new home. God's word says to live within your means. When you live within your means you live a life that is comfortable for you. You are not worried about keeping up with the Jones. You are not worried about what others may think or say about you. You do promise to leave a good impression of what others may say or think about you. Along with living within your means, God's word says to tithe and abundantly share. When you tithe and abundantly share you are obeying God's commands. You are tithing or giving the first ten percent of your income to God. This money does not belong to you. This money is God's money. It was God that gave you the job that you have made the money that you make. This is the reason we honor God with first ten percent of our income.

Malachi 3:10 (King James Version)
10Bring ye all the tithes into the storehouse, that there may be meat in mine house, and prove me now herewith, saith the LORD of hosts, if I will not open you the windows of heaven, and pour you out a blessing, that there shall not be room enough to receive it.

This is part of the plan that God has INS store for you. God promises to open up a window from heaven in which he will pour out blessings in which you will not have room enough to receive. God is a good God.

CHAPTER 5

Becoming At Peace With Your Spirit

As a Christian believer you must become at peace with yourself. When you are at peace with yourself, you are at peace with God. You can hear from God. You can hear the plans that God has in store for you. All, your heart, mind, body, soul and spirit are trying to become at peace with itself. Your spirit is tamed through the situations of the world and universe. Your spirit is looking to be feed. We feed our spirit through prayer, speaking in tongues, meditation, reading the bible, and worshipping God. Our spirit is longing for God. There is a peace that comes from within when you draw closer to God. When you know God. God is here for today, tomorrow, and forever. God says that he will never leave you no forsake you.

When you are not at peace with God you altar your spirit. The adversary attempts to do everything in his power to keep you away from the plans that God has in store for you. The adversary is trying to altar your spirit. The adversary knows that God has great things in store for you, which is the reason he tries' so hard to keep you from God's best. When you feel good about yourself, you feel good about the spirit you hold within. The people you associate with, the way you pray, your relationship with God. What you are doing on a daily basis. God's love for you will never change. You may be a person that has not known God in the past. You may be a person that has listened to the ways of the world. The world is trying to altar your spirit in which you do not have peace.

We practice mental meditation to become at peace. When you meditate on the good things you become at peace. Your body receives the nutritional fruit it needs to operate, survive, and thrive. When you feed your spirit you are giving your spirit the food that it needs. Your spirit operates off of the word of God. You build your spirit as you read the word of God. The word of God is the fruit of the spirit that feeds your soul. Your body needs this fruit in order to operate. When you read the word of God you know it. You become it. You become one with the body of Christ knowing the plans that God has in store for you.

The matters of the world are too much for you to handle alone which is the reason why we need God. We need God to get us through our days. We need God to guide us and show us the way. God looks out for you on spiritual base that involves advancing the kingdom of God towards the plans that God has in store for his kingdom. God's kingdom will prevail when Christ like believers believe that Jesus has died for them. We know that Jesus died so that you may have life and have it eternally in the kingdom of heaven. There is nothing the adversary can do keep you away from the plans that God has in store for you. The adversary will attempt to altar the plans that God has in store for you.

Depending on whether you are in a bad mood or good mood determines how your spirit will hold up. It determines how your spirit will operate. Your spirit is a conscious that exist which is feed through nutritional word of God that becomes stronger as you feed it. We feed our spirit to become stronger in the Lord. We become stronger in the Lord to know God's word, the plans that he has in store for us, and to allow us to complete a mission in Christ. God guides you through your spirit so that you know the plans that God has in store for you. All throughout the book we have been talking about the plans that God has in store for you. We know that our mission in life is to save life's through Romans 10:9, John 3:16, and John 6:47.

Romans 10:9 (King James Version)
9That if thou shalt confess with thy mouth the Lord Jesus, and shalt believe in thine heart that God hath raised him from the dead, thou shalt be saved.

John 3:16 (King James Version)
16For God so loved the world that he gave his only begotten Son, that whosoever believeth in him should not perish, but have everlasting life.

John 6:47 (King James Version)
47Verily, verily, I say unto you, He that believeth on me hath everlasting life.

When you believe that Jesus is your Lord you have everlasting life.

Becoming at peace with your spirit means becoming at peace with your heart, mind, body soul, and spirit. It means putting away those things that are foolish and evil.

1 Corinthians 13:11 (King James Version)
11When I was a child, I spake as a child, I understood as a child, I thought as a child: but when I became a man, I put away childish things.

As you become one with your spirit, your spirit matures. You put away those things that ate foolish or childish. You put away those things that keep you from God's best. The adversary, the world, and people will tempt you from being God's best. You need to become mature enough in the spirit that you can determine what is good for you and what is not. God allows you to know him as you build your spirit. As you build your spirit you grow closer to God. You build the relationship we have been talking about in this book. We are all seeking to build a relationship with God. Maybe you need someone to share your problems with.

Maybe you have been trying to go at life alone. Maybe you are depressed, down, out, or in misery. You cannot go at life alone. You need the help of all mighty God. God has great things in store for you. God loves you more than you can imagine. God wants to build a relationship with you. He is seeking to know you. He is seeking to answer your prayers. The love that you have for yourself is the love that you have for God. God's love runs deep. Its part of a seed that cannot be broken.

When you become at peace with yourself you learn what it means to meditate. You learn what it means to tame your spirit. It takes self-discipline to tame your spirit. It takes self-discipline to become at peace with yourself and learn the plans the God has in store for you. The adversary does not want you to make it.

1 Peter 5:8 (King James Version)
8Be sober, be vigilant; because your adversary the devil, as a roaring lion, walked about, seeking whom he may devour:

The adversary prides himself on taking advantage of those with a weak spirit. Those who do not truly know God. Those who have not taken the time to build a relationship with God. This is why you must grow to know God. When you are without God, your spirit is weak. You leave yourself open to experience heartache, pain, misery, and depression because your spirit is not yet mature enough to reject those negative matters, which present themselves.

When your spirit is mature throughout life and negative matters occur, your spirit automatically rejects them. Your spirit is in tune with the plans that God has for his kingdom. Your spirit knows what is healthy for it and what is not. Your spirit is seeking the procedure that God has in store for you. Your spirit is set to accomplish the goals, dreams, and ambitions that you have set for yourself. When you set these goals, you can follow through with a plan or purpose to allow you to reach your goals.

As your study and read the bible you become at peace with your spirit. Your body is feed the nourishment it needs to survive.

On a daily basis the world takes a lot out of your spirit. Your spirit feeds the occurrences of events that take place from the work that is put out into life. Our soul or spirit bleeds because it has come into existence with life. When your spirit is caught up in worldly matters it cannot operate to its full potential. You risk the chance of draining your spirit from the work that is put into life. This is why your spirit must be built on a daily basis.

The scriptures we read are healthy for our heart, mind, body, soul and spirit. The allow us to become complete. They allow us to become one with God and the plans that God has in store for us. In this book in the chapter spiritual intelligence we learn about a spiritual intelligence we hold which was given to us at birth. This spiritual intelligence allows us to know the difference between good and evil. It allows us to know the difference between right and wrong. God has given you a spirit so that you may be guided. Keeping your spirit at peace is important to you and important to God. It allows God to know you more. As you build a relationship with God your spirit becomes stronger. You overcome obstacles that once made you stumble. You defeat the adversary and break the curses of life. Curses of poverty, curses of money, family, friends, relationships, and abundance. The adversary try's to put a curse on your spirit, because he knows that you are part of a plan. Your spirit guides you towards the tactics that you should accomplish in life.

Your spirit allows you to meditate on higher things. When we discuss higher things, we are discussing situations, happenings, and believes that lead you to heaven. We are all trying to reach heaven, which is the reason we live our lives. We are looking to live a good life.

We build our spirit to help us get through our day. This is the reason we meditate on the scriptures of the word of God. These scriptures help us to know the plans that God has in store for you. You hold the power to control your destiny.

There are many false spirits throughout the world that attempt to convince you that their way of life is the way to live. These spirits know the greatness that you hold which is why they

Sean Maddox

try so hard to keep you away from God's best. The adversary try's hard to keep you away from God's best.

We develop a spirit within us from knowing God's word. God's word not only feed's our spirit, it guides us to our destiny. It keeps us away from those things that are not healthy for us throughout life. Having an unhealthy relationship with your self-leads to having an unhealthy spirit. This is why you grow to love yourself. When you love yourself you love God.

When you pray, you become at peace with your spirit. You allow yourself to meditate on the situations that occur throughout your life. You are able to let your request be known unto God.

Philippians 4:6 (King James Version)
6Be careful for nothing; but in every thing by prayer and supplication with thanksgiving let your requests be made known unto God.

This is why we go to God in prayer. We make our request known unto to God. There is only so much that man can do throughout the world. God needs for you to sit back and allow him to handle your situation. Sometimes you have to sit back and let God. Sometimes you have to let God in your situations. God can handle your problems better than you can. God knows what is best for you. God knows what you can handle and what you cannot. This is why God is seeking a relationship with you. God wants to know you. God is a good God.

CHAPTER 6

According To God's Plans

As a Christian believer, the plans that God has set for you must work out according to his plans. We know that God will not give us anything that we cannot handle in life. God's plans work out according to his plans because they must work out to specific plan or purpose. We often think that our plans are the best for our lives, but it is God's plans that are greater than our own. God has given you the power to achieve. No one said that it was going to be easy. No one said that life was going to be handed to you. You have to work for things that you want most out of life. Many people believe that life is unfair. Life is what you make it.

Everything happens in its due season.

Ecclesiastes 3:1 (King James Version)
1To every thing there is a season, and a time to every purpose under the heaven:

The reason your past has not worked out according to your plans because it is not your season yet. There is a season for everything. There is a purpose for everything. You must learn to work according to the plans of God. You cannot get discouraged when things are not working out according to your favor. God has a plan for your life.

Jeremiah 29:11 (King James Version)
11For I know the thoughts that I think toward you, saith the LORD, thoughts of peace, and not of evil, to give you an expected end.

God's plans for you to have an expected end or promising future. One that brings you great success, wealth, happiness, and laughter. Many people think since things have not worked out in the favor that God does not have a plan for them or God does not care about them. This is not true. God has not forgotten about you. God still loves you more than you can imagine. God knows that we mess up in life. We all make mistakes There is nothing to big to where our God will not forgive y our. You have to know who you are as a person. The moment you begin to know who you are the moment you begin to find yourself. You begin to learn about yourself. It may seem like your life is not working out according to your plans, but they are working out according to God's plans. We all go through different problems, different struggles, and different adversities. He knows that God has great things in store for you. You have to know who you are as a person. You have to know that you are a child of the highest God. You have to know that you have been called out before the foundation of the world to complete a mission through Christ. The is the reason for your existence in the world. You are not simply living to just live. You are living with a purpose. You are living to carry out a mission through Christ. We know that things might seem to get tough or hard in life. What is a life without pressure? Brainstorm things that you are good at. There are plenty of things that you are good at in life that you can make a career out of. Do what you love and you will never have to work a day in your life. We all have had a late start in life. We all have made mistakes. This is the reason why God forgives us. God knows that things do not always work out according to the way that we planned. This is why we go to God in prayer to hear the message that God has in store for us. There is nothing you haven't done that God would not forgive. This does not mean go out on purpose and commit sin only because you know God will forgive you. God forgives us out of mercy. God forgives you out of love. God has a love for you that stretches out further than you can imagine.

God may want you to join a church or prison ministry to support inmates. Whatever the reason may be it all works out according to his plans.

You can probably dream of the day you will have your dream home, dream car, and dream life. It has not happened yet because it is not its season to take place yet. Everything has its due season in which it will take place. God gives you life so that you may be fruitful and multiply.

Genesis 1:28 (King James Version)
28And God blessed them, and God said unto them, be fruitful, and multiply, and replenish the earth, and subdue it: and have dominion over the fish of the sea, and over the fowl of the air, and over every living thing that moved upon the earth.

God planned for you to replenish the earth. With God there is an overflow of abundance. God is not going to run out of resources. You have to know who you are. When you know whom you are you become at peace with yourself. You learn what you are capable of. What you can handle. God needs people that he can trust. People who will do the right thing.

You cannot force things to happen in your favor. You have to let things become natural. We know that you have a lot to offer the world. This is the reason in which God has created you. God wants you to share your gifts and talents with the world. God wants you to let your light shine. When you truly begin to know God you begin to know the love that God has for you. God's love will never fail. God will never stop loving you. It may seem as though God has not loved its because God has taken his hand of favor off of you through disobedience. This is why we must obey God in all that he has in store for us.

When you begin to build a relationship with God, you begin to know God. You begin to trust God and all that he has in store for you. All throughout this book we talk about building a relationship with God. God is looking to build a relationship with you. God did not plan for you to live in defeat. God did not plan for you to be broke, not having any money, not being healthy, and not living your life with a purpose. No, these are symptoms from the adversary. You have been blessed with a gift. Its time for you tap into the gift that God has given to use as part of your plan. The gifts and talents that you hold are part of you the plan that God has in store for you. You cannot worry about people who become jealous of you. The adversary in whom they cannot see that you are a child of the highest God blinds these people.

You must learn to keep your spirit in tune. When your spirit is in tune your lifeline up. The adversary will always tell you that you are less or that you are not good enough. He knows that you are closet to your breakthrough, which is the reason why he works so hard to keep you away from the plans that God has in store for you. You are special to God. God loves you. God has called you out before the foundation of the world to complete a mission in you. You cannot spend your life worrying about other people's problems. Remember other people's problems are their own problems. God has given you your own life to worry about.

God brings those special people along your path to get you to your destination. People that will push you. These people have an affect on our lives. They change our lives for the better. They come into our lives and give us the motivation that we need. They make us feel good about ourselves. They make us feel like we want to do well for our lives. We see what they have and it allows us to know that we can do it also. These people never come off in the sense that their bragging, but that they have been blessed by all mighty God for carrying out the purpose and mission that God has placed in their life. God has made it this way so that they might be together. So that they might be a part of a team.

Everyone wants to feel complete. As if they are part of a purpose or higher calling. Maybe you are in a field that does not bring you much joy. Millions of people are in a field they do not love. They have allowed themselves to participate in something that does not bring them God's best. When this occurs you cannot receive God's best. You need to be in a field that you love. A field that brings you great joy. When you do the things you love it feels as if you are not working because you enjoy them so much. The adversary will always try to talk you out of it. But God has something greater in store for you.

My books are written to bring you closer to God. To help you find your true destiny, purpose, and mission in life. Many people who read these books have never truly known Jesus. They have lived their life according to their plans and according to a worldly sense instead of the plans that God has in store for them.

When you live your life according to God's plans things work out according for the better. Life flows with the evolution of life and all it has to offer. Life has so much to offer. God has something greater in store for you. As you begin to know yourself you begin to know God. You put away those things of the world and focus on those things of God.

You are closet to your victory which is the reason the adversary is fighting you so hard. God wants you to know that he still has plan for your life and it all starts with you. It all starts with you making the decision that you are going to live your life for God. You cannot worry about the ways of the world. The reality shows, the arguments you have with your husband or wife. You have to leave those things up to God to handle. God has a way of moving people out of your life that do not need to be there. God will bring you people along your path that will brighten your day allowing you to reach your destiny.

Learn to sit down and have conversation with God. God is seeking to speak with you. When you begin to build your relationship with God, you begin to make a friend. A friend that will be there for you through thick and thin. God has the people in your life that will help to complete your destiny. From my own

Sean Maddox

experiences in life I can look back and see how God has taken people out of my life that were meant for harm and brought people in my life to bless me. God see's what you need in your life. God has not forgotten about you. God is simply waiting for that due season. There are many things that you are good at in life that we take for granted or we do not use on an everyday basis. Why let our talents go to waste? You can use your talents to bless people in ways you never thought possible. In the same way you are blessing yourself because you are using the gifts that God has given you to complete the plans that God has in store for you.

He will always convince you that you are not good enough, but God says different. Use the talents that God has given to complete the plans that he has in store for you. God helps those people that draw closer to him. Do not worry about the ways of the world. The world will always try to deceive you. Put your faith in God not the world. Man alone cannot guide you to your destiny. When you get tired of the world whopping your tail you will draw closer to God and the plans that he has in store for you. God has something special in store for you when you believe. The problem with most people is they stop believing. They do not believe that God has something in store for them. They set back and become passive because they do not see their dreams coming to life. Life takes ambition, dedication, determination, commitment, and scarf ice. You have to be willing to role with the punches. You have to be willing to play the hand that has been dealt to you. We all have a hand that was dealt to us, its up to you what you do with it.

Will you change your life and start living you life for God. We are in a spiritual battle between good and evil. It will take your believing to change the world around. It will take more philanthropy, more volunteering, more going to church, and more tithing, more reading the bible, more praying. The angels are rejoicing in heaven. They are cheering you on so that you might make the right choices in life. God still has a plan for your life. Do not let the adversary deceive away from your dreams. God is still completing a good work in you. You can believe that you are part of a destiny. You must believe this with all of your heart. Your mind is the most powerful asset you own. Start training your mind to do those things that you know is right. God loves you more than you can imagine. God is a good God.

CHAPTER 7

Let Your Light Shine

As a Christian believer. God needs for you to let your light shine bright. God has given you light to illuminate the world. The world is filled with darkness, corruption, and evil spirits in which corrupt the world. The adversary lurks around the world seeking to devour whom he can.

1 Peter 5:8 (King James Version)
8Be sober, be vigilant; because your adversary the devil, as a roaring lion, walketh about, seeking whom he may devour:

The adversary preys on the weak. Those with weak minds. Those who are in the dark. Those people who are away from the plans that God have in store for them. The adversary knows that if he can control your mind, he can control you, keeping you away from the plans that God has in store for you. This is why you must keep a strong mind. God has let your light shine so that you might illuminate the world. God needs for you to bring let to the world.

Matthew 5:16 (King James Version)
16Let you're light so shine before men, that they may see your good works, and glorify your Father which is in heaven.

God wants you to illuminate the world. There are plenty of dark places throughout the world the need the light of God. There are plenty of people that need the light of God. Millions of Christians throughout the world need the light of God. God brings people in your life to bring light into your life.

1 John 1:5 (King James Version)
5This then is the message, which we have heard of him, and declare unto you, that God is light, and in him is no darkness at all.

The light that you hold guides your heart, mind, body, soul, and spirit to the plans that God has for them. God gives you what you need and will not give you more than you can handle.

The bible holds the light that you need to teach to the world. This is the reason God tells us to go out into the world preaching the gospel to every creature.

Mark 16:15 (King James Version)
15And he said unto them, Go ye into the entire world, and preach the gospel to creatures.

The world with no light is a dangerous place. God is not able to show his hand of favor upon those he loves the most. The adversary attempts to keep you away from the light. He knows you are less powerful when you are away from the light. The light is too bright for those non-believers. It goes against their will in what they believe in. The adversary tries to blind you with his own light. This reason God has given us a spiritual intelligence to determine the difference between the values of the light that is being illuminated to the world. God gives you light as gift to shine into the world. God gives you light, because he trusts that you will do the right thing with it. You will let your light shine so bright before the world to see. The light in which you hold is empowering. It shines, illuminates, and guides you through the ways of the world. When you are in darkness you fear the world.

This why God has given you light so that you will not fear. Fear is a spirit of the adversary. God gave you no fear.

Psalm 23:4 (King James Version)
4Yea, though I walk through the valley of the shadow of death, I will fear no evil: for thou art with me; thy rod and thy staff they comfort me.

God has equipped you with no fear. God did not create you to fear those things of the adversary. You can rise up in the strength of Christ knowing that you are an overcomer. The light of God brings a lot of people to God. God's light shines so bright. The adversary hates to see you with the power of God. This is the reason why he tries to keep you from reaching God's best or the plans that God has in store for you. God constantly allows his light to shine bright.

When you are in the dark, you are away from the plans that God has in store for you. God cannot talk to you. God cannot communicate with you. You begin to walk down the wrong path listening to the wrong plans. This is the adversaries way of controlling you into believing the lies in which he pitches. The adversary never gives up in which he tries to sell your soul. The adversary does not care about your life. He just cares about selling your soul. This is the reason why this book is so powerful. This is the reason why have saved your life so that you may not sell your soul to the devil. All throughout this book there are scriptures written to surrender your life to Christ. This gives you the opportunity to surrender your life to Christ knowing that Jesus died for your sin so that you may have eternal life. The adversary loves to attack your family, friends, fortune, heart, mind, body, soul, and spirit. This is the reason why you must guard your heart, mind, body, soul, and spirit. The adversary knows if he can control your mind he can control you.

The light given to you were given to you to make the earth shine. The earth was corrupt. It belonged to the adversary since he was cast down from heaven. The earth becomes corrupted and dark. This is the reason you have light. This is the reason God allows you light to shine. When you read the bible, pray, and meditate you allow your light to shine in to the world. This is why we witness to others. We witness to others to show our love for God as we are spreading the love of God. Completing your plan for God takes time. It takes discipline. Its takes love. The light that you have attracts people around you. This is the reason why people like you. They are attracted to the light that you hold within you. God has given you this light as a gift to share with the world, so that you may tell the world about Jesus. Jesus will come back for all who believe in him so that they may have eternal life. God is coming back for his people. God wants you to tell the world about him. This is the light that you hold that you share with the world. God will not give you more than you can handle which is why he has given you a mission in life. God has allowed you to know him more. God has allowed you to know his plans. When you begin to follow the light, you begin to know God. The problem with darkness is you don't know what comes with. It comes blind. It comes deceiving. It does not tell you all the evil spirits about it. It leaves you in the dark to where you are now blinded by the allure of the wrong light. Everything the glitters are not gold. You have to be strong enough to know who you are as a person. You have to be strong enough to make the right decision throughout the kingdom. God trusts you to complete a mission in life. God knows that he can complete a mission in you throughout life.

You could be part of a bigger plan. You could be the reason why someone commits his or her life to Christ. God may use the light that you hold to bring someone closer to God. Life is not a game to be played. Life is what you make it. There are plenty of people that have been left in the dark. People who have been left to not see the plans, purpose, and mission that God has in store for them. The problem is our believing is too small. We allow our minds to become filled with I cant do it mentality that we dwell on that and live it. Our mind is more powerful that you can imagine. That's why the mind is terrible thing to waste. God has given you light to shine into the world, which is the reason people see, the light in you. This is the reason people are attracted to you. People see the light that you hold and are attracted to it. People need that same deliverance. No one can rob you of your light in which you hold. The adversary fights hard to steal the light you hold away. The adversary attempts to keep you in the dark. This is the reason you must be strong in your heart, mind, body, soul, and spirit. The adversary tries to learn your ways. He attempts to teach you pleasures and your desires. He then attempts to take them away from you. This is how the adversary tries to leave you weak. God is more powerful than you can imagine. This is the reason why God loves you so much. God will not give you anything that will hurt you. God will never leave you nor for sake you.

Hebrews 13:5 (King James Version)
5Let your conversation is without covetousness; and is content with such things as ye have: for he hath said, I will never leave thee, nor forsake thee.

The light you hold is special to the kingdom of God. It illuminates the kingdom of God. You have to believe in the light that you hold. It is more powerful than you think. It helps to guide the way of your heart, mind, body, soul, and spirit throughout the kingdom. You have already been equipped with the spirit. Spirit that you need to get you through your day. God has allowed you to go in those places that need light to complete a mission through Christ. There are lives that need to be saved out there and you hold the power to save lives. God has given you the power to save lives. Do not worry about what others may say or think of you. Remember to always leave a good impression on others and what they may say.

The light you hold brings a peace among you that only God can bring. The adversary will attempt to come in many forms keeping you away from God's best or the plans that God has in store for you. God needs for you to love him. God needs for you bless those people around you. You have been blessed with gifts.

Things that you are good at. God needs for you to use those gifts to bless that people in your life. It makes no since to let your gifts go to waste throughout the kingdom. Their great sacrifice given to the light that is given to you. You must sacrifice yourself to carry out the plans that God has in store for you. God knows what best for you. God knows what you need. This is the reason we pay attention to what God is saying and not the world. If we listened to the world all day we would never hear the plans that God has in store for us. God brings you up from t he position that you in. You have to start viewing yourself as smart. You have to start viewing yourself as creative. The moment you view yourself as both smart and creative the moment you begin to tap into the power that you hold. God has given you this power for a reason. God has given you this power to change lives. You hold the power to change lives. You hold the power to save lives. You do not have to live in a trap your whole life. You do not have to listen to the adversary. You are a child of the highest God. Do not listen to the lies of the adversary. God loves you. Jesus loves you. Your family loves you. This is the love that God has for you. You can call on God for anything. God wants you to do those things that you know are right in your heart. There is a peace that comes within you when you are doing those things that are right in the eyes of God. God wants you to be a part of plan. A higher calling. You are special to God, which is the reason why he loves you so much. God is good God.

CHAPTER 8

Patience

Through patience you will find that your dreams will come true. Your opportunity comes with the patience that you have for God. Work according to Gods plans. In the bible it says lean not until thy own understanding.

Proverbs 3:5 (New King James Version)
5 Trust in the LORD with all your heart, and lean not on your own understanding;

As a Christian believer this may be hard. Leaning not until thy own understanding will be hard at first. You will he use to operating in your own form of method. You will be use to doing things your way. As a Christian believer you have to allow yourself the opportunity to doing things God's way. God has a certain method of performing his tasks. A certain method of operating that allows one to reach his goals. You are a child of the highest God. You are operating out of the nature and admiration of the Lord.

When you lean not until thy own understanding you choose to perform in God's method. You choose to perform in God's way instead of the ways of the world. The world will try to transform you into their methods, which are not the way of God. Remember you are not of this world. You were simply put in this world temporarily for a mission. In the twenty first century world that we live in there are to many lost corrupted souls in the world. When we discuss lost corrupted souls, we are discussing the importance of souls that have been lost. Souls that have been corrupted by wrong governments, poor politics, poor leaders, false God's, false prophets, wrongful idolatry, idols, celebrities and adversaries. This is the world the adversary attempts to feed you to keep you away from the plans that God has in store for you. The adversary will feed you these lies because they seem good on the outside. We must warn you to stay way from these people in which they will do you harm in your walk with the Lord and your faith. You must take the time to master your faith.

When we discuss mastering your faith we are discussing the importance of keen craftsmanship in perfect obedience to the Lord thy God. When you are obedient to God, you practice Proverbs 3:5 where it discuss lean not until thy own understanding. It takes character to display perfect obedience to the plans that God has in store for you. Whether you believe it or not God has a plan for your life and the people around you. We discuss the vast number of individuals who have been distant from God. The vast number of individuals who are afraid to come back to the kingdom of God. These individuals have messed up in life and feel there is no forgiveness for their sins, which is simply not true. God is extremely remorseful for forgiving one of their sins. No matter what it is that you have done, God still loves you. God is ready to build a lasting relationship with you and the people around you. God is ready to show up and show out in your life.

You are special to God. You are part of a seed that God has planted in your life in which he plans to plant in the lives of others across the world. A seed that is planted in you that cannot be taken away from no one. The adversary is out to kill steal and destroy.

John 10:10 (New King James Version)
10 The thief does not come except to steal, and to kill, and to destroy. I have come that they may have life, and that they may have *it* more abundantly.

Sean Maddox

The adversary's main goal is to sell your soul. Your soul belongs to God because you are saved. You may be thinking I do not know if I am saved are not. Here is scripture that will allow your soul to belong to the kingdom of God in which you will go to heaven and have eternal life.

Romans 10:9 (New King James Version)
9 that if you confess with your mouth the Lord Jesus and believe in your heart that God has raised Him from the dead, you will be saved.

Romans 10:9 discusses of the importance of having Jesus Christ as your Lord and savior. The scripture discussing the importance of Jesus dyeing on the cross for your sins. Jesus' blood was shed on the cross for your sins, so that you may be free from sin and free from the adversary when he attacks. When your believe that Jesus died on the cross with all your heart you are confessing that Jesus is your Lord and savior and that Jesus died for you so that you may have eternal life in heaven. No matter where you are with your walk with the Lord, you can grow closer to God. The late bloomer was written to highlight those people in life that have had a late start. People who feel they have been left out, forgotten, or not cared for. The late bloomer is the person in life that has blossomed late in life in which God has not forgotten about them.

In the world that we live in now, we want things now. We want things to happen right away. We work hard for things that we have in life. We want things right away and we feel that we should have them. Its part of a conscious that eats at our soul that we continue to feed with the energy that we put into life. You learn to work the well without working thirst till you die. This means you begin to find out what works well for you and you become good at it. Sure you will try and fail at many different alternative options until we get the job done, but that's part of the life that we currently live in. In the day and age that we live in everybody wants things to happen now. People want the millionaire status, the big homes, cars, clothes, jewelry, mansions, and possessions that make one feel good about the accomplishments that one has set out to achieve. Do we really need all these things to make us happy? Some do, some don't. Regardless of how many personal possessions you own God still loves you the same. God loves you more than you can imagine. He loves you unconditionally and his love for you will never change.

The focus of this chapter is patience. In life everything will not always be cookies and cream. In life you have your ups and downs, peaks and valley, high and lows, storms and valley, downfalls and ups. This is part of the life that we live in. You have to learn to be patient for things that you want out of life. Everything does not always happen when you want it to happen. Try telling that to kid that wants it now. We live in a very bold and vibrant environment where kids are not accustomed to the fears of the world. Kids are very bold these days and there set out to achieve the goals, desires, dreams, and ambitions that they want to achieve. Kids are very talents and their great at using their talents to better achieve themselves. One problem individuals are not successful is because there in a field that does not have to do with their talents. You have to recognize your talents, goals, dreams, and desires and execute on them to the best of your ability. This problem of not knowing what your good at actually happens later in life. Older adults are stuck in fields they hate, don't enjoy, or would rather be doing something else. They have not taken the time to maximize the criteria they specialize in use their talents to better themselves and the people around them. God has given you talents. Everyone has something that they are good at. God designed everyone this way. These are the talents that you should be using to your advantage so that you can better the people around you. Great people make the people around him so better. This is why Michael Jordan was so great and still is a great person to this day. This is why he is considered one of the greatest basketball players to ever play the game because when he went to work he made the people around him better. It wasn't that he went out and won the game by himself. No it was team effort and Michael made the people around him better by simply being himself.

Many people are afraid of being themselves. They try to hide under an alternate identity that defines everyone but himself or herself. This is part of being patient. When you are patient you find yourself. Find your true self. You find who you are as a person and what you stand for. Finding yourself of who you are as a person and what you stand for. So many kids today are caught up in the world in which they worship celebrities, false God's and false prophets. The world has blinded our kids. The adversary has blinded our kids. We must guard the material that we are putting out into the world in which we feed our kids minds. The saying a mind is a terrible thing to waste is so true.

You have to be able to multi task. God will not give you more than you can handle. God gives you what you can handle. God gives you all that you need. Its up to you to reach out and make your dreams come to life.

Through patience you find yourself. God molds you. God is continuing to mold you into the form or life that you now live in. You find what works. Presentation is important in the way that you present yourself. You're able to present yourself in professional way through preparation. Preparation is the key and you find that through patience.

God loves insight. God loves your input. God is ready to here from you. He loves your thoughts, ideas, dreams, goals, desires, and ambitions. God is ready to build a lasting relationship with you. God is ready to know you. Of coarse God knows you because he created you, but God is ready to know you on a personal level. Be who God created you to be.

Wondered how successful people made it. What do they have that I don't. Why are they luckier than me? Why are they more blessed than me? I found that you have to find your hustlers spirit. We all have a hustler spirit inside of us. We all have an ambition that allows us to push ourselves to the next level. We all are trying to reach that next level in life and you should push to achieve the necessary goals that will thrust you to the next level. The devil doesn't want you to make it. We all are under attack by the adversary. The late bloomer was written to help you grow closer to God. It was written to allow one to know that God is continuing to work on you and you will reach your desired goals when the time is right. God is never late. My aunt always told me that God would line everything up. Sure enough, God lined everything up. Everything came into play. It all came into action. Everything must workout according to God's plans. You cannot rush God; it must work out according through his plans. You learn this through patience. We talked about how God molds you into a born again believer that allows you to know that you are saved through Jesus' blood that was shed on the cross for your sins. You will find that the mold allows you to become mature. It allows you to find yourself as a person. Most importantly it allows you to become complete as a person. Becoming complete as a person is a part of finding yourself. It knows that God has something great in store for you. We all have thought it at one time or another that God has something great in store for us. Its something that we feel, its something that we know, its something that makes us feels complete as a person. God is looking to build a relationship with you. Will you let him? Will you grow with Christ? Will you allow your love to blossom? God is a good God.

CHAPTER 9

Blessings Right Around The Corner

As a Christian believer, you continue to believe the goodness in which God has in store for you. God is a God of abundance. God is a God of peace. God is a God of overflow in an abundance of opportunity. You have to know that your blessings are right around the corner. God has blessings with your name on it. You have to know that God has blessings with your name on it.

As a Christian believer you may feel as though you have not received blessings in the past or even received any blessings, but that is all about to change now that you have found God! The adversary has blocked your blessings in the past to which you could not receive them. The adversary has attempted to keep you away from the kingdom of God. God brings you to new levels in your life. God is constantly trying to push you to new levels. God does not want you to get comfortable throughout life. God wants you to stretch out your faith to carefully blend with the plans that God has in store for you. God continues to bring you to new levels. God takes you away from places that he doesn't want you to be exposed to. The adversary attempts to take hold of you blinding you giving you impaired vision for the sight that God has in store for you keeping you away from your blessings. The adversary attempts to keep you so busy that you will not receive the blessings that God has in store for you.

As a Christian believer in order to receive your blessings you must not ever lose your respect that you have for God. Continue to go to church. Continue to show God that you truly love him. As a Christian believer you must learn to find time for God. You must learn to allow yourself to be open to the many opportunities that God has in store for you. God is ready to do great things with you. See blessings are not only receiving them. God is ready to do a work through you. God is ready to allow you to be a blessing to others. Its great to know that you can be a blessing to others. God is ready to poor out a blessing in which you will not have room enough to receive.

Malachi 3:10 (King James Version)
10Bring ye all the tithes into the storehouse, that there may be meat in mine house, and prove me now herewith, saith the LORD of hosts, if I will not open you the windows of heaven, and pour you out a blessing, that there shall not be room enough to receive it.

God commands us to bring our tithes to the storehouse in which they are stored. God promises to open a window from heaven and pour out blessings in which we will not have room enough to receive.

Acts 20:35 (King James Version)
35I have showed you all things, how that so laboring ye ought to support the weak, and to remember the words of the Lord Jesus, how he said, It is more blessed to give than to receive.

In this verse God is displaying the importance of giving. It is important t give more than it is to receive. In giving you trust the value of what you have inherited to bless others with. You may be a person in which giving comes natural or easy to you. God encourages you to continue to give from your heart. When you give, you give from your heart. You show that you are responsible enough to receive blessings in which God has blessed you with that you are ready to bless others with. God trust you with the blessings in which you have received in which God has granted you with. God also looks at the you have done with the blessings in which he has trust you with. God is looking at what you have done with the past blessings that he has blessed you with in the past. How did you inherit them? What did you do what them? How did you bless others back? How are you thankful for the blessings that God has blessed you with? All of these factors come into play with the blessings that you receive. God is looking to bless those who are faithful to him. Those who listen. Those who use the gifts that God have blessed them with to bless others with. You might feel as though you have not received any blessings in the past, but that is all about to change. God is ready to bless you with an overflow of abundance. God is not going to run out of blessings. God is not in a recession. The only recession is in our mind! To often we limit our mind. We put a recession on our mind. God is recession proof and so are you. God is a good God. God is a God of overflow of abundance.

When you are in line to receive your blessing the kingdom of God will come in line. Everything will be right on track. God prepares you to receive. The adversary attacks your blessings so you cannot achieve. The adversary attacks your finances because he knows this is subject that is close to your heart. A subject that is a necessity of life. A means of living that is greatly needed to achieve success in the sense of wealth.

When God spoke to me about writing a book, I thought to myself I'm going to touch people's lives, touch their lives. I had no financing, no television time, no New York time bestsellers, no promotions, no advances, no way of convincing executives that I qualified to sell New York time bestsellers under my name. All I had was an agreement with God to write the best books that I possibly could to touch people's lives.

I love to write books. I receive ideas, inspiration, topics, messages, and daily devotion from going to church. I sometimes go 3 or 4 times a week to receive all that I can from the messages. The messages from God really touch my heart. I always receive so much from messages from Joel Osteen, Jessie Duplantis, Tim Story, Walter Hallam, Rick Warren, Creflo Dollar, Kenneth Copeland, Paula White, and Bill Winston at I store into my blessing account. I look at these guys and I think to myself these guys are great. These guys are really amazing. They inspire me so much. They were put here on the face of the earth to do the will of God. God always has a way of putting the message through other people to get to you. When you receive your blessings their will always be people around you that need blessings as well. This is why God has blessed you. God wants you to be blessings to those around you that have not received their blessings.

Proverbs 13:22 (King James Version)
22A good man loveth an inheritance to his children's children: and the wealth of the sinner is laid up for the just.

God has a way of speaking to you. This is part of a blessing that God has instilled within you. The blessings that you receive are an act of love.

God has blessed you with gifts through life and the kingdom of God to bless others with. Gifts to bless family, friends, relatives, wives, and co-workers. God has so much in store for you. There are so many blessings with your name on it. Blessings that are stored up in the kingdom of heaven that you will receive when you get there. I have a wonderful scripture to share with you about storing blessings.

Matthew 6:20 (King James Version)
20But lay up for you treasures in heaven, where neither moth nor rust doth corrupt, and where thieves do not break through nor steal:

God is saying to store treasures for you in heaven rather than upon earth in which these treasures will last forever. God has already layed out treasure for you in heaven in which you will receive when you get there.

John 14:2 (King James Version)
2In my Father's house are many mansions: if it were not so, I would have told you. I go to prepare a place for you.

These are the blessings that God has stored up for you. You receive blessings from keeping a pure heart. God is able to bless you when he sees that you are doing right. Never become intoxicated with your blessings, wealth, and success.

We all have a story to tell. The story that you tell is part of your testimony. We all have a testimony to share. Blessings are given for you. You start to trust the blessings that you receive.

Wealth is more than money. Wealth is a state of mind. Wealth starts with a mind set. It starts with the way that you view yourself. How do you see yourself? What type of goals do you have for yourself? Where do you plan to see yourself in five years? How will you get there? What do you plan to do to get there? These aspects all come into factor with your state of mind. The adversary loves to attack you in your mind. He loves to keep you away from the plans that God has in store for you. You have to keep a positive mindset. You have to keep the mindset that you can do it. You cannot give in to the adversary when he attacks. The adversary knows that you have something special. Something that God has given to you as a gift that you may cherish as an investment into your wealth, which is your state of mind. You cannot acquire wealth without first having a state of mind. Your state of mind enables you to receive blessings. This is why a state of mind collaborates with blessings. Better to be rich in good works than good investments. Be good with the things that God has blessed you with.

You have to learn to train your state of mind to acquire wealth through blessings. IF you have a poor state of mind, then you will be a poor person. If you have a rich or wealth state of mind, you will be a rich person. Your state of mind is powerful beyond measure. We often are afraid of our own state of mind that will cannot achieve what we have set out to achieve throughout life. The fear is embedded in us through the adversary. The fear that you have is not from God, it is a fear from the adversary. The adversary attempts to instill fear in you in which keeps you away from the destiny in which you have set out to achieve. This is why we must guard our heart, mind, body soul, and spirit. You must guard your state of mind. Your state of mind likes a vault because it gives access to the very treasures that you hold. You have the power to achieve more than you thought possible. To often we limit ourselves. Limit yourself through fear of what is to come. We allow the adversary to come into our lives, controlling our very destiny. You have to be able to tap into your state of mind at all times.

Keeping your mind free from negativity is important. Your mindset cannot afford to be clogged from negative debris of your problems and other people's problems. You are a child of the highest God. God has set you out before the foundation of the world. You have been equipped with all that you need to succeed in life. God is ready to open up the windows to heaven and pour out blessings in which you will not have room enough to receive. As a Christian believer, you have to be ready to receive them. You have to be bold enough to say that this is your time to receive the blessings that God has in store for you.

CHAPTER 10

Hustler Spirit

As a Christian believer you have a hustler spirit inside of you. You hold the power to amass the necessities that you want out of life. Life is passing you by. What are you going to do about it? How are you gong to react? What is the life that you plan to build for yourself? How do you view yourself? How have you changed? Ask yourself these questions. You have the power to hustle. Life is what you make it and how will you make yours? What do you plan to do with your life?

You may feel that you have not amounted to much in life, but that is not true. You have your health, strength, wisdom, and age. God has blessed you with wonderful gifts. You have to work towards the gift of taking nothing and making something out of your life. This relates to your creativity in life. How do you view your creativity? How are you creativity? In what ways has God set you apart from others throughout life? God gives you the power to manifest your destiny. God gives the power to be somebody. This book is written to help you inspire to be all that you can be. Maybe you have been holding back in the past. Maybe you have been lazy. God is about to change all that. You have the power to get wealth. You hold the power to control your destiny and do not let anyone tell you different. Many people try to hold you back in the past because they feel they cannot do something.

They see you doing something with your life and they want to try to keep you away from the plans that God has in store for you. What are you doing with the life that God has given you? Are you going to simply sit back and not make something of yourself or are you going to make the most of your situation. How are you playing the hand that was dealt you? How do you plan to live forth in abundance? You have the power to control your destiny and no one else.

God is ready to work miracles in your life. You may have failed in the past, but did you stop there? Did you quit? Did you give in to the devils temptations? God has something special in store for you. Millions of people throughout the world are growing closer to God as we speak. We are living in times in which the adversary does not want us to grow close to God. The adversary does not want us to make it. God has plans that are different. God has plans for you to prosper. God has plans for you to succeed.

Learn to build the hustler spirit inside of you. Learn about yourself. Learn what it takes to make it in the world. How are you going to react to world that both doesn't and does care about you? How are treating the people in your circle of friends. Examine the people in your circle of friends that you have for yourself. Maybe your friends have let you down in the past. Maybe your friends have talked behind your back. Told lies about you or mistreated you throughout life. How will you react to this treatment? You do not have to settle for less. You are a child of the highest God. God loves you more than you can imagine.

Begin to examine the gifts, talents, and traits that you are good at. What is God telling you? How is your relationship with God? What is God telling you? What are the plans that God has in store for your life? What treasures are you storing up in heaven?

Matthew 6:20 (King James Version)
20But lay up for you treasures in heaven, where neither moth nor rust doth corrupt, and where thieves do not break through nor steal:

God is saying to store up treasures in heaven rather than upon earth. The treasures that you have for yourself in heaven are eternal meaning they last forever. Treasures upon earth are simply temporarily. Tap into your hustler's spirit. Find what it is that you are good at. What are your talents? How has God blessed you in ways that will allow you to prosper and help prosper others?

How do you react to rejection? Do you simply give up? Do you try harder? Do you tell yourself that you are somebody and that you can make it throughout life? Life is a gift. Life was granted to you through Jesus Christ. We know that Jesus died for our sins so that we might be saved throughout the world. If you didn't know it, you know now. Jesus died for your sins so that you might be saved and free from sin throughout the world. You now live above the curse. You live above the curse of poverty, the curse of religion, politics, sports, health, and fitness. The adversary attempts to put a curse on you to keep you locked in to the powers in which he stores to hold you back. The adversary attempts to keep you trapped. You do not have to live this way.

We know that success comes with hard work, motivation, and determination. In order to be successful, you have to view yourself as successful. You have to examine yourself. Examine your character. Examine what others are saying about you. Success is a state of mind. Your mind is your most powerful asset. You have the power to be anyone you want to be.

A hustler's spirit is God given. Have it or you don't. There is no in between. There is no right or wrong in the eyes of a hustler. It's a part of the hustle. It's a part of your demeanor. The way you were raised or brought up. It's the sacrificing that you have to make in life. You hold the ability to work miracles. Ability to believe in God. Ability to make something of yourself. The ability to prove others wrong when individuals say that you are not anyone.

Sure you will have downfalls. Sure you will have pressure, but what's a life without pressure right? You are an overcomer.

You are a child of the highest God. An individual set apart from the world.

Your hustler spirit is what the world is saying about you. What are the conversations that go on about you? Are they good? Are they bad? Are they inspiring? Are they motivating?

What do you do what the money in which is placed in your hands? What do you do with the resources that are in your environment that God has blessed you? Everywhere you look there are places in your environment that you can reach out to pull yourself up.

Your hustler spirit is your swag. It's the conversations that people discuss about you. It's the way people look at you. The way people view you. The way people look up to you. There is so much creativity in becoming a hustler or defining yourself. You discover new talents that you never thought that you had possible. It's the people that are in your circle. The people you relate to. The people you get along with and the ones you call your enemies. The saying keep your enemies close is true.

How do you dress? Are you dressing for success or are you setting yourself up for failure? What are you doing for the people around you in your environment? Are you lending a hand? Are you being a servant for the Lord? Are you setting an example through Christ? People look up to you. You have something special. People want to be around you. They see the things that you have done and they want to be just like you. You draw people closer to you, but you are really drawing people closer to God.

How are you reacting when things get tough? What are doing when you starving and you have no way to eat? How are coaching the people around you? Are you uplifting them? Are you inspiring them? Are you teaching them? It is known that in oriental cultures a teacher is one of the highest honors. A person that is greatly respected. Sure there are ball players who are paid millions of dollars throughout the world for their talents, but think about all of the under paid teachers who contribute and are responsible for the great success of students who go out and

Sean Maddox

make it in the real world. These teachers have a great reward in heaven!

How are you adapting to change? What questions are you asking yourself? Get use to a lot of questions? When you begin to find yourself, you find that you will be overwhelmed with the amount of questions that you will have for yourself. How do you react to bad news? Are you calm under stressful situations? Money is the number one cause of stress. You have to be able to say calm under stressful situations. What are you saying about yourself? How do you view yourself? What are people saying about you? What do you do when your demeanor is under attack? How do you react?

Who are your heroes? How are you heroic? You have the ability to change lives. You have the ability to control your future. Begin to change your state of mind. Begin to change what you are saying about yourself. Start thinking positive thoughts. Start to feel good about yourself and what you are doing.

How do you bounce back from a fall? How do you pick yourself back up? These things occur throughout life in which you should be prepared for them. Do not waste time. Start to think of yourself as successful. See yourself in that brand new car. See yourself in that brand new home. See yourself getting married. See yourself going to church more. Find yourself. My friend when you find yourself, you find success. You find the reason in which you exist or the reason in which God has created you. We know that God has created us for something. We do not simply exist for any reason. God has plan and a special purpose for you life. Continue to do those things that you know are right. God is a good God.

How do you react when the devil attacks? Do you study the word of God? Do you pray? Do you see yourself in others especially successful people? Do you see yourself in others who aren't doing well for themselves? In what ways can you improve yourself? What are you doing when you find that you have yourself in a bind? Are you teaching others around you? These topics need to be addressed. They need to be discussed for the forward progression of the movement that is going on in your community. What do you stand for? Are you covering every angel that you cannot leave any room for the adversary to come in? Do you find yourself going in circle throughout life? Why is that? What can you do different? How is the adversary attacking you? Remember when the adversary attacks you throughout life is because you are closet to your victory. You have the power to overcome. You have the power to block out negative thoughts that come your way.

Are you leading star or supporting role type of person. You might feel that too are a star, but you really are a supporting role person. You work best alongside someone in which you work together to get the job done.

When developing your state of mind, it's important to eat healthy. It's important to take good care of your body. Your mind works of the foods in which you store into your body. You cannot think or function if you are not eating the foods that are healthy for you. Are the foods that you enjoy the best foods for you? Are they healthy for you? This is an important aspect to developing your state of mind. DO not let anyone altar or influence your state of mind. You obtain complete control over your state of mind. You have the ability to control your destiny and no one else. You have a hustler spirit inside of you. Its what you do. Its how you feel. It's the way that you view yourself and others.

God has been continually working on your state of mind in which he completes a work in you. God wants you to develop a state of mind that comes second to none. A way of life. An evolution to life. Its part of which you are. How you view yourself says a lot about the person that you are. You may ask, where does all this come from? It comes from experience. It comes from doing the right thing. Listening to God. Putting in a full day of work. Trusting God that the plans that he has in store for you are better than your own. There is a wealth of abundance in your spirit. You must be in tune with the right spirit. The adversary will attempt to persuade you believe his ways. He will offer you riches and wealth which look good on the inside, but leave you feeling lonely or worse lead to you selling your soul to the devil. Your soul belongs to God, you are saved. The scripture Romans 10:9 allows you to be saved know that you know that Jesus died so that you may be saved.

Romans 10:9 (King James Version)
9That if thou shalt confess with thy mouth the Lord Jesus, and shalt believe in thine heart that God hath raised him from the dead, thou shalt be saved.

This scripture saves lives. It keeps you from selling your soul to the devil in which you become a slave to his works. You are child of the highest God in which you do the works of the Lord. You are a servant of the Lord in the respect that you treat others the way that you want to be treated. God has great things in store for you. Lift the heavy burden off of you. Keep the devil out of you life. God has great things in store for you. God is a good God.

CHAPTER 11

Spiritual Intelligence

You have been equipped with a spiritual intelligence. God has allowed you to know his presents through a believe that comes from within. God has allowed you to know him all, because he is the God that we serve. He is the God that we know. The person we have grown to believe in. God has a plan for your life and it all starts with you.

The spiritual intelligence that you have helps to define the person you are. God planned for you to know him more. God planned for you to use the spiritual intelligence that he had given you to help those around you. There is nothing the adversary can do to take the spiritual intelligence that God has given you away from you. God planned for you to be with him. God planned for you to know him, to know his ways, and to know his word. We study God's word to become closer to him. The spiritual intelligence that God has given you is given to you at birth. It is acquired through the creation of mankind for mankind.

The spiritual intelligence you hold cannot be taken away from you. Its part of a seed that cannot be broken. God created you so that you may be more like him. The spiritual intelligence you have holds meaning to the creations of the world.

The spiritual intelligence you hold is part of a network. We are all connected in the body of Christ. We are Christ like in every way since we belong to God. God gives us spiritual intelligence to know him more. Before you were born or before you were saved you had no spiritual intelligence. You did know the ways of God. You were simply conformed to the ways of the world. You did not know God. You did not know of God. You simply existed in the world as not a born again believer in Christ.

When you are born again you are saved through Christ. You know the ways of Christ. You know the plans that God has in store for you. You are equipped with a spiritual intelligence that cannot be broken. God created you to be more like him in you exist because God created you. God created you to be more like him in every way. God equipped you with a spiritual intelligence so that you may know him more, but more importantly know his ways. God has a plan for your life. The plan for your life all starts with you. It starts with excepting Jesus as your Lord and savior. When you accept Jesus as your Lord and savior you surrender your life to Christ. As you accept Jesus as your Lord and savior you are given a spiritual intelligence, because you are now born again. You know believe in Christ. You believe that Jesus is your Lord and Jesus died for your sins. Jesus' blood was shed on the cross for your sins. This is the reason we give communion at church. We are showing respect by acknowledging the sacrifice the Jesus made for dying on the cross for us. Jesus died for you. Jesus died so that you may have life eternal in the kingdom of heaven.

You may tame your spirit by going to God in prayer. Your spirit is a part of you. It's a part of the reason why God created you. The spirit you hold allows you to become humble. We humble ourselves to humble more people. The spirit that God has given you allows you distinguish the difference between good and evil. Some call this spirit your conscious. Your spirit is feed by the situations that occur throughout your life. God comes in the form of a spirit. This is the reason that God still exist in you. You are part of the spirit of God. You are part of the body of Christ. God's spirit remains over you through the storms of life.

The spirit you have within you is one the remains close to God. God made you one with him. He created you to be Christ like. God says he will never leave you nor forsake you.

The spiritual intelligence you hold allows you to be made known unto God.

Romans 1:11 (King James Version)
11For I long to see you, that I may impart unto you some spiritual gift, to the end ye may be established;

This is the spiritual gift that the Lord gives you. Its part of a gift that last forever. There is nothing anyone can do to take away the gift that God has given you. That gift cannot be taken or broken.

The spiritual intelligence you hold is given to you so that you may put it into work. Faith without works is dead.

James 2:26 (King James Version)
26For as the body without the spirit is dead, so faith without works is dead also.

God created you to be one with him, which is the reason God, has given you a spiritual intelligence. God allows you to know him more. In fact, God wants to know you more. He wants his spirit to rain down deep amongst you.

The adversary will always try to altar the spirit that you have with God. Your spirit is part of a seed. A seed that has been planted within you from the day you were born. This seed is feed through your spirit. Your spirit feeds and nourishes the spirit in which you hold. This is why the seed you hold needs the spirit of God. The spirit of God runs deep throughout you. It is held within you so that because God loves you. There is nothing man can do to take the spirit in which you hold away from you. This spirit belongs to God not man.

Sean Maddox

The spirit you hold is part of a true power. A power you hold from within. That spirit that you have comes from within. The spirit that you have is life. God gives you spirit so that you may have life. So that you may be apart of something. No one wants to feel left out. No one wants to feel like they are less. God completes us through spirit.

The spirit that you hold is the same spirit of all mighty God. It is a spirit in which you can worship God. It is a spirit in which you may know God more. The spirit you hold may come in a variety of shapes and sizes. Some small, some big, some thick, some vapor. It's a part of a connection you hold with God that God has given to you. Remember life is a gift and should be treated as one. You belong to the body of Christ. You are a Christ like believer through Jesus. Your spirit can be tamed.

Before you had your spirit you did not know God. You did not know the ways of God. You only knew the ways of the world. You were brought into the world to complete a mission through Christ. You are a Christ like believer in the name of your son Jesus Christ. God has called you out before the foundation of the world to complete a mission in you. You were created with purpose. You were created for a mission.

The spirit you hold is key to knowing God. It allows you to become one with God. Your spirit belongs to God. It is meant for no harm. It's created so that you may know God more.

You look to build your spirit as you become closer to God. The reason God gave you a spirit is so that you may be one with him. The adversary is out to keep you away from God's spirit. The adversary will try to ruin your spirit. God wants you to live a life that is honoring to him. God's plan for you is to succeed in life. God does not want you to go around defeated. God planned for you to prosper.

Your spirit is part of an important creation in which God has created to feel the earth. God's spirit runs deep. Your spirit is holy. Its part of a gift inside of us that God has given to us accomplishes great things.

It's important to keep harmful people away from your spirit. Your spirit must be protected. If you allow the wrong people access to your spirit you risk the chance of altering your spirit in the sense that is becomes weaker. God has made you stronger with him.

Ephesians 6:10 (King James Version)
10Finally, my brethren, be strong in the Lord, and in the power of his might.

God wants you to be stronger in him. He wants you to know him more.

When your spirit is stronger you feel more complete towards the plans that God has in store for you. We become closer to God so that we may know him more. So that we may know his word more.

The spirit you hold within you is brought to you through the Lord. When you surrender your life to Christ, you became one with the Lord. You allowed yourself the opportunity to trade in all your sorrow for eternal life throughout he kingdom of God. We keep our spirit up by worshiping God. We choose to worship God; we are not forced to worship him. It is our free will choice to worship God.

We are at a constant battle between spirits. The battle between good and evil. It has been this way since day one. We battle within our spirits to gain authority over matters.

Your spirit matures over time, as you become more of Christian. As you draw closer to God you truly learn what it means to have a spirit and how to become one with Christ. God will not give you anything that you cannot handle.

You cannot change the life that God has given to you. God has given you that life for a reason. God has given you that life so that you may use it more abundantly. To many times we abuse the life that was given to us. The spirit that you hold with you is life. It's a part of the life that God has given to you. God has given you life because he loves you.

Why did God create me with a spirit? God created you with a spirit, because he wanted you to be one with him. He wanted you to be a part of something greater. Something epic. Something special. You are a part of something special to God. You cannot change who you are. God created you that way because he wanted you to exist in that manner.

It is not always easy to live your life for God. The reason God gave you a spirit is because he knew that he was created something of great stamina.

God created you because he loves you. He knew that you would be part of his plan. He knew that he could count you to complete the mission and purpose for which is exist. You are not simply living your life for the hell of it. You are living your life through Christ. You are living your life with a mission and purpose to serve God.

God's spirit can be neither shaken nor stirred. It simply remains constant. It is the variable. It is part of the reason in which you exist.

When you have a spirit within God you grow to know God more. We know God more through our spirit. Our spirit helps to define us. It shows us who we are. It shows us what we stand for. God's spirit continues to grow. It grows with the people around you. It grows with the people in your community.

Your spirit networks with other Christ like believers to complete a mission through Christ. Your spirit is part of a network that belongs to God. A network that is established to make up the kingdom of God. God allows you to draw closer to him as your get to know him.

Many people are living their life to the world's standards. They have not grown to know Christ. Christ has so much to offer. There is so much you cannot do when you are not saved.

The spirit of God remains in you today, tomorrow, and forever. As we grow closer to God, we know God more. We know more of precious love, the fruits of the spirit, and that entire God has to offer.

The world is filled with artificial spirits, false God's and false prophets. This is the reason we must draw closer to God daily. We must know God more and more and the plans that God has in store for us. God's word is full of his love. It fills our spirits daily, as we know him more.

Believing in the spirit of God allows you become free. Free from burden, free from strife, and free from the troubles of the world. You may feel your heart is troubled. Its only because you have tried to live a life without God. You have tried to make things happen with the help of God. You must life your life through Christ. You must live for the plans that God has in store for you.

There will be many spirits that try to come as false prophets, false God's and false witnesses. God's love for you will remain the same forever. It will never change. God continues to bring you closer to him.

The spirit that you have within is not altered by the ways of the world. God has already equipped you with breaks that will boast you to the next level of your life. You do not have to worry about where your breaks will come from.

God's spirit is a part of who you are. It's a part of the way you were created. You were created for God. You were created to be Christ like. You were created to know God more. God has great things in store for you. God is a good God.

CHAPTER 12

Taking Nothing and Making Something

To survive in this world you have to be able to take nothing and make something out of it. These are your survival skills. Your survival mentality. You were born with it. Its skills that you acquired at birth. You hold the power to your success. As a Christian believer you have to believe. You have to believe there is a way when there is no way. You begin to develop something from within. A believe that is formed through knowing God. When you know God you become complete through Christ. You live your days in the Lord for Christ and no one else.

What are you going to do with the life that was given to you? Remember that life is gift and should be treated as one. God has granted you the gift of life in which you should do everything in your favor to honor God.

When you take nothing and make something you turn over a new leaf. You remember everything that was told of you from day one. God loves you more than you can imagine. Its part of the love that God has for you. God's love for you will never change. It will remain constant. It will remain in you till the day that you die. The love that you have for yourself is the love that you have for God. We know that God loves us. We know that God will always be there for you through thick and through thin.

What instincts are you developing within yourself that you can use to your advantage? What are you saying about yourself? What are others saying about you? What are you doing with the time that has been given to you? God enables you to know more of his love. More of the plans that he has in store for you. We continually talk about the plans that God has in store for us because they are important. They are part of who we are. Its what we do.

The survival skills you acquire allow you to enhance your ability to make it in the real world. This is a real world that we live in. Are you ready for it? Are you ready for change? Are you ready for the change that is taking place?

You may have come from the dirt. You may have acquired wealth through the forward transfer of family income. Some of you have not yet reached that level of success, but will soon get there. Do not give up on God. Do not give up on yourself. God created you specifically for a purpose. God created you to walk and talk like Christ. You are Christ like in which you are saved through Christ. The attitude that you have for yourself is a reflection of the forward progressive state of the mindset that you have grown accustomed to. You live your life according to the way that you feel. The way that you views others and what others may be saying about you. How do you view your life? What are the goals that you have set for yourself? In what ways have you tried to improve yourself? You may have lived life on both side of the fence, but God is still finishing a good work in you.

God loves to prove himself. God loves to show out. God's love for you never fails. It continues to out do itself time and time again. When you love God you love yourself and when you love yourself you love God. This is the way God planned it to be. God planned for you to live in victory over defeat of the adversary. The adversary comes to kill, steal, and destroy.

God continues to prove himself time and time again. Lets examine the way that you view yourself. Do you view yourself with love? Are you treating others the way they want to be treated? Love the people around you? In what ways are these questions affected you life for the better? In what ways have these methods hurt you? Ask yourself, am I really putting my all into life. Taking nothing and making something requires you to put your all into life. It requires you to be the man or woman that God created you to be. Are you living your life to the fullest? Are you doing everything in your power to help the people around you? If not, why are you living? You are not living to simply exist for no reason. You are living to draw the attention of all mighty God. Everywhere you go millions of people are growing closer to God and the plans that God has in store for them.

God brings you out the pit that you are in. God lifts you to a new level or new perspective towards the way life is viewed. Becoming one with God is part of the process of knowing who you are as a person.

Developing your believe from within comes from knowing God. It comes from building a relationship with God and the people around you. Get to know God. Learn the steps, objectives, and tasks that God has in store for you. Why is it everywhere you go people cant seems to get enough of God? People are seeking God daily. They want to get know God more and more and the numbers show it. The numbers show it from the number of mega churches that are being formed. Everywhere you look there are a number of churches that are being formed. People are pulling to closer to God by record numbers. People draw closer to what it is that they like. What they can relate to. People love God and the numbers show it.

God's love for you never fails. It never tarnishes. It remains one with you, as you are one with it. Continue to do those things that you know are right. Continue to build the people up around you. They need it more than you think. People need the love of God, which is why they are turning to God. People are coming closer to God because they know its God that they can trust. They know that God will never leave them nor forsake them.

Hebrews 13:5 (King James Version)
5Let your conversation is without covetousness; and is content with such things as ye have: for he hath said, I will never leave thee, nor forsake thee.

This is a promise from God. The bible is filled with promised through his word. Let your actions be known unto God. Let God know what it is that you are trying to accomplish throughout life. When you live a life without God, you live a life that is destined for failure. It is hard to live a life without God and expect positive results that will boast you to the next level. God continues to prove himself.

Ask yourself have you done this before? Have you lived a life that is honoring to God? Have you done everything in your power to serve the Lord thy God? Why wouldn't you want to serve the Lord? Why wouldn't you want to work with God? What is holding you back from accomplishing your dreams, your goals, and your destiny? Its destiny that we are all looking for. Its destiny that we are attempting to chase. Life comes and it goes. Eternal life last forever. Eternal life is the key factor to living for Christ. It is no secret that you love God. There are millions of Christians that love God. The key question is are they living a Christian life that is honoring to God. Are they pleasing God? But most importantly are they saved? It is up to you save lives. God has given you the gift to save lives. Romans 10:9 allow you to save lives. It's a simple scripture, but it is important to God.

Romans 10:9 (King James Version)
9That if thou shalt confess with thy mouth the Lord Jesus, and shalt believe in thine heart that God hath raised him from the dead, thou shalt be saved.

When you confess this scripture you are confessing the Jesus is your Lord and savior. You are confessing that Jesus died for you sins so that you may be saved through Christ.

Taking nothing and making something requires you to use your mind. We continually talk about the importance of using your mind. A mind is terrible thing to waste. This statement remains true. It is one that viewed as a way of living. A way to acquire the necessities of life. God allows you to become one with him. God allows you to know him. What is it that God is saying about you? How do you view yourself? In what ways are you trying to improve yourself?

Taking nothing and making something requires you to improve yourself. It requires you improve the person that you are, the person you will be, and the person you become. Becoming a better you is allows you to know yourself. We all are looking to know ourselves. God has great things in store for you when you believe.

You did not get to where you are in life alone. You did it with help. You did it with the help of the people around you. You used resources to help you get to the point that you are in life. What resources have you used to help you accomplish your dreams? In what ways have you bettered yourself? How have you tried to make a difference in the world that you live in? God continues to complete a good work in you.

Philippians 1:6 (New Living Translation)
6 And I am certain that God, who began the good work within you, will continue his work until it is finally finished on the day when Christ Jesus returns.

God promises to finish the work that was done in you. You are part of plan for God. You are part of the plans that God has in store for you. We know that God has great things in store for us through the scripture Jeremiah 29:11.

Jeremiah 29:11 (King James Version)
11For I know the thoughts that I think toward you, saith the LORD, thoughts of peace, and not of evil, to give you an expected end.

These are the plans that God has in store for you. God has nothing but God things in store for you. You are apart of God. You are apart of a treasure. A treasure that is stored in heaven. God continues to reveal the plans that he has in store for you are you grow closer to him. Continue to do those things that you know are right. Continue to do those things in the eyes of God. You are honoring God. You are living your life in commitment to Christ.

God only ask that you listen. Listening to God is important. It's also needed to take nothing and make something. You have to develop listening skills. You have to listen to the people around you that God has placed in your life. God continues to place people in your life that will uplift you. These are the people in your life that will bring you to new levels. You cannot worry about what others may say or think of you. Worry about what God is saying about you. Worry about how you want to see yourself successful in the years to come.

You must learn to see with your eyes. How do you view the people around you? How have the people around you helped you to see a clearer vision? What is the vision that you have for yourself? God is curious to know. God wants to know more about you. He wants to help you. God is ready to thrust you to a new level if you are ready. You have to be able to push yourself. Allow yourself to develop into the mold that God has set for you. We develop a mold for ourselves through listening to God and seeing ourselves achieving the success that we want to achieve. We all want to achieve success and we will in our due time. Everything happens in its due season.

Ecclesiastes 3
1 To every thing there is a season, and a time to every purpose under the heaven:

This is the purpose in which God operates. Everything has its due season or due time. All of the kingdom of God falls into place when one is in alignment and harmony with the plans that God has in store for you. We know that God has great things in store for you. God is a good God.

CHAPTER 13

2 Close Mindedness vs Open Mindedness

As a Christian believer, you must learn to keep an open mind towards what the world has to offer. God has created you specifically for a reason. God created you with a plan.

When you have a closed mind you miss the plans that God has in store for you. You miss the key points that God is trying to show you in life.

God has a plan for you life and it requires you to keep an open mind. God has plans for your life and it requires staying open to plans that God has in store for you. We know that God's plans are greater than our own. God will not give you anything that you cannot handle.

When you have an open mind, you can hear from God. You can hear the plans that God has in store for you. All, God is seeking to speak to you, but it requires you to keep an open mind. God needs for you stay open to ideas, concepts, and believes that he has in store for you, rather than the plans that you have in store for yourself. To often throughout the kingdom of Go, people are keeping a closed mind towards the ideas, plans, and concepts that God has in store for them. When you have a closed mind, you limit your ability to revive the very best that God has to offer. God has so much to offer. The adversary will try to keep you away from the plans that God has in store for you. When you have a closed mind, you cannot hear from God. You miss the plans that God has in store for you. God is seeking to communicate with you daily, but if you do not keep an open mind, you cannot hear from God. You cannot hear the plans that God has in store for you.

People with open minds were born that way, but it can be acquired over time. God gives you an open mind, because he wants you to revive from him. He wants you to receive the plans that he has in store for you. God's word is the truth. It's the way we define our life. It's the way that we live our life. God would not have given you life if he didn't love you. It's all a part of the plans that God has in store for you.

Open-minded people listen to God. They listen to the plans that God has in store for them. They are not worried about what others may say about them, because they know that God has them in the palm of his hands. God sets the agenda. God call the shots. We all belong to the body of Christ in which God has created us. God created us to be more like him in everyway. We exist because God loves us. We exist as part of a greater calling. Part of plan. Part of a purpose. God created you to have an open mind to be more open to the possibilities that God has created.

When God gives you an open mind, he does it to complete a work in you. God does it to tell you the plans that he has in store for you. God would not give you an open mind if he didn't think that he could trust you with the plans that he has in store for you. To often we keep a closed mind, ignoring the very things that God is trying to tell us. We shrink back in fear, scared of the realities of the real world. The mind that was given to you was given to you to use to think of others with. God needs you to put the mind that was given to you to use. The mind is terrible thing to waste, which is the reason you should work so hard to put it to good use. Your mind is a creation given to you by God used to control the way that you think. You control the way you operate through your mind. God did not create you without first knowing that he had a plan for your life. It all started with you. It all started with God creating you for a higher purpose. A higher calling. A calling that would complete the kingdom of God and plans that God had in store for you. This is the reason God has created you. This is the reason in which you exist.

Your mind was created so that you may use it to think. God needs you to use your mind to control the realities of your life that occur. Your body cannot operate without it, meaning it is a basic function of life. God knows that you are part of his creation. You are part of his masterpiece. God created you to be one like him. When God spoke the world into existence, we became one with him. We became part of his plan in which we were in one accord with the plans that God has in store for us.

When you keep an open mind you can hear that plans that God has in store for you rather than keeping a closed mind. Closed-minded people cannot hear from God in which they ignore the message that God has in store for them. When you have closed mind, God speaks to you, but you simply ignore him. You do not operate in the spirit of God, because you have not yet matured in your spirit. You have not yet grown to know God and the plans that he has in store for you yet. God is seeking to speak to you everyday. No often we keep a closed mind and miss the message that God has in store for us. We often think that our plans are greater than the plans that God has in store for us and we miss the plans that God has in store us. God's word never goes void. It is constant it is the variable that is set.

An open-minded person grows to learn more from God. An open-minded person seeks God. Open-minded people look for more of what God has in store for them. They do not attempt to live their life to their own standards in which they ignore the plans that God has in store for them or try to live plans that go according to their standards. When you agree to live for God, you agree to live your life according to the plans of God. These are the plans that God has in store for you. You may not believe that God has a plan for your life, but he does. God loves you more than you can imagine. God has a plan for your life. God's plan for your life consists of you accepting Jesus as your Lord and savior. If you are person that does not know Jesus, this book has been written so that you may know God. This book is written so that you may know that Jesus is your Lord and savior in whom you become a born again Christian knowing that Jesus blood was shed on the cross for your sins. Jesus died for you. Jesus died that you may have life and have it eternally. You exist because Jesus saved you. Jesus saved you from the ways of the world so that you may live above the curse. You are free from the curse. You are free from sin. You do not have to live in defeat anymore. You can live knowing that Jesus died for your sins in which you are saved from the sins of the world.

When you keep an open mind your open to new ideas. You can hear from others people. Many reasons peoples ideas fail or the reason people run out of ideas is because they have kept a closed mind towards the ideas, concepts, and plans that God has in store for them. God is always trying to speak to you. The problem is people keep a closed mind towards the ideas, plans, and concepts that God has in store for them. People feel the way they are living is satisfying enough so they do not listen to the plans that God has in store for them. People feel they come to point to where they cannot learn anymore. They feel no one else can teach them anything, which hurts their point of view towards life. You need to learn to respect people's opinions from alternative perspectives. You can learn some much in life when you keep an open mind towards things. Life has so much to teach you. The greatest lessons learned in life are lessons learned from life not school. Its life where you learn to blossom into the man or woman that God wants you to be. You cannot get through life trying to learn everything on your own. You need the help of people. You need the help of the people that God created. God created us to help one another throughout life. God did not plan for us to be alone.

Genesis 2:18 (King James Version)
18And the LORD God said, it is not good that the man should be alone; I will make him a helpmeet for him.

God created you to be with the creations that he created. This is why we have an open mind towards life. We are open to the new ideas, believes, and perspectives that God has created because we grow with the evolution of life. Life evolves from alternative perspective as we progress. If it did not, we would die. We would not live the fluent lifestyles we have grown accustomed to know.

God created you with an open mind because he wants to show you more. He wants you to continue to grow towards the plans that he has in store for you. Closed-minded people have set a tone in their mind that they cannot receive more of what God has in store for them. They think and feel as though they must operate on their own in which they become solo thinkers. Often times, people have become hurt in their past which is the reason in which they have become closed minded. They do not allow hurt due to their past to influence their life because they have been let down in the past by rejection. The pain and the agony of what they feel will not allow them to feel more pain. They become closed minded towards the ideas, plans, and concepts that God has in store for them that they miss the message that God has in store for them. This way of thinking hurts them because God cannot communicate to them. The communication process does not flow fluently towards the ideas and concepts that God has in store for them.

They do not allow themselves to trust again because they have been burnt in the past. Trust because an issue of hurtful remembrance towards them because they have failed to keep an open perspective towards the ideas, plans, and concepts that God has in store for them. All though one may keep a closed mind, one begins to believe in him more because of the trust that is lost in others as they grow to love. They grow to love themselves more first, before growing to love the world again.

When keeping an open mind you learn to appreciate the efforts of others. You learn to appreciate what others are doing for you on an outside perspective. God allows you to keep an open mind to know him more. God is looking to grow closer to you. To build a relationship with you.

When you keep an open mind you learn to methods about yourself. You learn what your capable of. You learn your guidelines, boundaries, and borders. God will not give you anything that you cannot handle. God gives you just what you need. God see's your efforts. He see's that you are trying to do something with your life. When you live a life that is complete, you live a life that is for God. You are not worried about the ideas, concepts, and plans of the people around you. Other people do not faze you. You learn to live your life for yourself instead of others. We all know that the adversary is out to kill, steal, and destroy. The adversary is trying to keep you away from the plans that God has in store for you. This is the reason the adversary tries so hard to keep you away from God.

Living your life with an open mind requires you to be patient towards the ideas, concepts and plans of the people in your direct environment. God places people in your life that will boast you to a new level. People that will challenge your perspective. People that will bring the best out of you God will not harm you. God is looking to help you reach your goals in life. If God is for you, who dare be against you.

Romans 8:31 (King James Version)
31What shall we then say to these things? If God be for us, who can be against us?

God is one who has your back. He is one to not let you down. There is no one that can stand against you.

An open-minded person is one who listens to God. One who responds to the plans that God is telling you. When you keep an open mind you listen to the things that God is telling you. God is seeking to communicate with you on a daily basis, its up to you to keep an open mind towards that ideas, believes, and concepts that God is telling you. Will you be the one to listen to what God is telling you? Will you be the one to respond to your call? We all have a calling in life. Your calling is the reason in which you exist. It is the reason in which God has created you. God created you to complete your calling in life. As a Christian believer, you must complete you calling in life. You calling are your mission in life. It's the reason you live your life with purpose. God needs you to complete your calling. Will you complete the call? God is a good God.

CHAPTER 14

Observing and Appreciating Your Surroundings

As a Christian believer, it's important to observe your surroundings in your environment. Your surroundings are full of quality information, entertainment, guidelines, and outlines that will help you to reach a level of success that you are looking to reach. You can observe, gain, and learn so much from paying attention to people, places, and things around you. Your level of work increases as you hone in on the skills portrayed by people related to your industry. The problem with most is they attempt to live a life on their own. They attempt to do things on their own. We cannot operate in this world alone. God planned for us to multiply and be fruitful. God did not plan for us to be alone.

Genesis 2:18 (King James Version)
18And the LORD God said, it is not good that the man should be alone; I will make him a helpmeet for him.

Genesis 1:28 (King James Version)
28And God blessed them, and God said unto them, be fruitful, and multiply, and replenish the earth, and subdue it: and have

dominion over the fish of the sea, and over the fowl of the air, and over every living thing that moveth upon the earth.

First God tells us that it is not good for man to be alone. God planned for us to be fruitful and to multiply the face of the earth. God planned for the earth to replenish in life so that we may have life eternal.

Rejoice in what the Lord has given you. You have so much to be thankful for. When you appreciate those things in your environment you appreciate the entire Lord has done for you. You appreciate the love, joy, peace, patience, and victory that God has given you. To often we are unappreciative of the things that God has given us. We go about our everyday lives without first thanking God for the blessings that we have received on a daily basis. God blesses us in ways that hold their weight in gold. You have your health, strength, and ability to love. God gives you the basic necessities of life because its what you need the most to survive. God gives you more as you ask for them.

When you appreciate your surrounding you appreciate the resources that are in your environment. Too many people go through life feeling they do not have the resources they need to achieve their goals. God has given you a great big world to choose from with plenty of resources. God gives you family, friends, money, education, health, religion, believe, happiness, joy, and laughter. These are the basic of needs that God gives you as resources to choose from. When you observe and appreciate the surroundings in your environment you appreciate what God has given you. You do not let the creations of the world go to waste. God is seeking to speak to you on daily basis and it all starts with you observing and appreciating your surroundings. It starts with you taking notice in the creations of the universe that God has created. The creations in the universe created by God hold power. They hold value. They're worth their weight in gold. This is why God wants you to be appreciative of those things. God wants you to be thankful for what he has given you. You can learn so much from sitting and observing. It was once said that the loudest one in the room is the weakest one in the room. Silence is golden. When you sit and observe you gain a personal advantage. This is the reason why God has given us two ears and one mouth. God wants us to listen more than we speak. We you listen or observe with your eyes you witness matters you would not have detected when you are busy going about your everyday daily routine of life.

God has so much in store for you. It all starts with you observing the surroundings in your environment. You can learn so much from observation. You learn what it is that God is communicating to you. You cannot hear from God when you are to busy for him. God is patient with you. He continues to communicate his plans towards your life even when you are not listening. The world speaks to you. The world displays its ability to offer you something to your personal advantage. When you observe you hone in on your skills. You examine what it is in your life that you need. You find the missing links or parts of your life. During your examination period you find that there are parts that are missing to your life. You take time to find what is missing and begin to find ways to fill them in. There are parts of your life that are missing, because you are too busy to have all of your life complete to the point that there is nothing else to do. Life is like a puzzle. You are always searching for the missing link to fulfill your life. You are always putting the next piece together to complete your life. The key to completing to puzzle is finding similar matches, occurrences, personalities, or objectives that relate closest to you, your walk with the Lord, and God to complete the puzzle.

There are certain things that you cannot learn on your own. Some things must be learned through simple observation. The process of your attention span to a certain task. When you go through life there are certain obstacles in which you will face that you have never faced before. Your body is not immune to these obstacles to which it has difficult time adapting to these new challenging occurrences. Your body or brain needs the help of an example or alternative that has already been through these occurrences. You must take the time to observe people, places, and things that have gone through these examples that can leave the footprints in the sand for you to follow. Your body's natural reaction is to pay attention to people who have come before you. People who have paved the way for you to bloom into the person that you have grown to be. People like Martin Luther King who stood up for civil rights. People like Barrack Obama who paved the way for African American Presidents. People like George Washington who led the way for all presidents. These people have faced those obstacles in life that we have not faced. You cannot sit back in complain about what you don't have. Complaining will not get you anything. You have to go out a make a difference in the world. God has placed you in this world for a reason. God has placed you in this world to make a difference. You have to learn what it means to sacrifice your life. Jesus sacrificed his life for you when he died on the cross. The adversary will always do everything in his power to keep you away from the plans that God has in store for you. You have to be strong enough to know that God has something greater in store for you than the ways of the world. The world may seem tempting to the eye, but the world often lies and deceives man. This is the way of the adversary in which he operates. He is clever, cunning, and deceiving in the sense that he keeps you away from what God has in store for you.

God needs for you to appreciate people who have paved the way for you. In today's world especially with the youth, to many people do not appreciate what people have done for them. What elders have done for them? What legends have done for them? What parents have done for them? Youth go through life expecting everything to be handed to them. In life you have to make something of yourself. Nobody is going to hand you anything. You must put the work in behind it. You have the ability to achieve anything and everything that you want to achieve. God has given you a great big world to choose from as a platform or your personal playground. The possibilities are endless.

We know that God is trying to speak to us on daily basis. God is trying to gain your attention so that you might know the plans that he has in store for you. You cannot continue to go about your daily activities ignoring the Lord and expect to receive the results that God has in store for you.

When you sit and observe you are patient. When you sit and observe you take the time to learn new avenues. New outcomes or possibilities that life lead you towards. God does not want you to get comfortable. God wants you to continue to grow. When you are not growing, you are not operating in the fruit of the spirit. The world has so much to offer you. God wants you to use those gifts in which he has given you to the best of your ability to advance the kingdom of God.

The problem with some people is they feel they have to work to hard for things that they want in life. There pretty much is not way around working for the thing you acquire unless you inherited some wealth, which is the reason you should be working in the first pave. You are not simply working for personal gain alone. You are working to leave an inheritance to your children and children's children.

Proverbs 13:22 (King James Version)
22A good man loveth an inheritance to his children's children: and the wealth of the sinner is laid up for the just.

It gives you great pleasure to leave such great wealth to someone you love. It allows one to feel as if there work on earth is appreciated. You are always growing in life. You grow so that you advance the kingdom of God. If you did not grow, you would become dead. You would not evolve.

God allows us to share life with one another for a reason. You develop new life as you share with others. When you observe from others, you learn the avenues in which they went to achieve their success. It does not mean that you are trying to be like them, but you are attempting to set the tone for foundation of success that you are seeking to achieve. You learn to appreciate opinions, ideas, and objectives of other people's agendas that have proven track record in a given industry or field. Their people will help

Sean Maddox

you become responsible for your success. Imagine attempting to enter a new field or industry without any help. You can imagine the frustration one must feel without seeking the proper help of an individual throughout life. God gives you help because you need it. God gives you help because he loves you and he doesn't want to see you without it. If you are person that seems to have your life perfectly together, why don't you try to help someone get their life together if you have not already have. God will place you in their life for a reason, so that you might help that person get to their next stage in life.

Observation is a gift given to you by God. It allows you to obtain skills in which you did not previously have to better enhance your skills in a certain field or industry. The next time you are in the grocery store or department store, browse some of the isles that of your favorite products. You can learn so much from reading the descriptions of the product. Where the product is manufactured? Where the company is located? What the product has to offer? This observation allows you to learn more about the products that you love.

You can learn a lot from observing a woman. Women in life pretty much have their stuff together. You do not have to talk a whole lot when it comes to women. Women will tell you her heart. All you have to do is set in listen. This all comes from the gift of observation in which God has given you. God allows you to observe to better yourself. God allows you to observe so that you might continue to grow in life. God does not want you to get stuck in life. He wants you to continue to grow in life. You do not have to go the route the everyone else is going. You can set your own tone. You can have your own agenda towards certain outcomes, situations, and alternatives towards life. God has allowed you to observe for a reason. Use your five senses of touching, tasting, smelling, seeing, and hearing to observe certain areas in your environment or atmosphere. Continue to better yourself. Continue to love yourself. God is good God.

CHAPTER 15

Using The Resources God Placed In Your Environment

God has placed resources in your environment for a reason. God has placed resources in your environment so you may use for your advantage, but most importantly to advance the kingdom of God. To many people do not take advantage of the resources that God has placed in their environment. God has given them to you so that you may use. God has given them to you as gifts. God blesses you with gifts so that you may use. Everywhere you look, God has given you the resources that you need to achieve the goals that you need. You must learn to believe in yourself. You must learn to believe that you can achieve. The problem with most people is that they stop believing in themselves. They lose the believe that God once gave them as a gift in the first place. They allow the adversary to come into their lives and control their destiny. We know that it is not healthy to live in this world alone. God has given you people in your life as gifts, but most importantly as resources so that you might reach out to in times of need. People all around you in your resource field are there to help you reach your goals every step of the way. You might feel there are not enough resources in your environment, but you are not searching hard enough. God places people in your life for a reason. God places people in your life to help you reach that next step or goal that you are looking to achieve. You cannot let people tell you that you cannot achieve or that you are not good enough to live the career or life that you want. People that tell you that you cannot achieve say this because they see the gift that God has placed on the inside of you and they are jealous that they do not hold these same gifts. In return, people keep you away from God's best. They hold you back or keep you down. We want what God wants for you. We want God's best for you. You can receive God's very best for you by using the resources that God has placed in your life. There are number of ways to find resources in your environment that will help you achieve your goals. Search within the schools that you have attended in the past. Schools are filled with talented productive people from all walks of life that have so much to offer the world. People who are talented in arts, acting, history, drama, sports, clubs, and mentors. Some of the same people that you went to school with or currently go to school with you will need later in life. Some of the same nerds that were laughed at by the class become the world millionaires. Simply look at all those computer geeks from the 60's and 70's who spent their time programming computer technology when the world's attention was focused elsewhere. There craft took time, but when the fan hit it hit. The 90's were spent in an era known as the Dot. com bubble or an area or field in the industry when computers introduced the Internet to the world on a massive rating scale. You should never be ashamed of the gifts that God has given you. Who knew these high school and college nerds would be the future visionary leaders of our world. God takes ordinary people and uses them in extraordinary ways.

When you begin to tap into the resources that God has given you, you begin to feel a peace on the inside of you. You that you are living your life out towards the plans that God has put in your heart. God gives you dreams for a reason. You do not have dreams in your heart for no apparent reason. They are important for your life. They are important for your destiny. Your dreams are part of the plan that God has in store for you. God needs for you to live your dreams out to the fullest. He would not have given you the dreams if he did not need for you to live them out to best of your ability. You need to be sure that you are that you are living your dreams out to the best of your ability and not wasting them. God is going to ask you, what did you do with the gifts that I have given you throughout the life that was granted to you. You do not want to say that you wasted the gifts and the talents that God has given you. You want God to be able to say that you work is done.

Matthew 25:23 (King James Version)
23His lord said unto him, well done, good and faithful servant; thou hast been faithful over a few things, I will make thee ruler over many things: enter thou into the joy of thy lord.

We are all connected in one accord. This is why we must use the resources in our field to help accomplish the goals, dreams, and desires of our hearts that God has given us. Are you living your life to the best of your ability? Are you living your life for God? Are you doing everything in your power to take advantage of the people, places and things that God has placed in your life? God would not give you the resources if he did not want you to have them. God is constantly pushing you to new levels. We continually talk about the importance of not getting comfortable in the position that you are currently in. God wants you to continue to grow. He wants you to mature. This is part of the book The Late Bloomer. As any good wine, you mature as life goes on.

To often we try to do things on our own. We try to make things happen without the resources that God has placed in our life. The reason things do not work out in your favor is because they are meant to be used with the company of more than one resource. God loves to work in groups or teams. He loves abundance. This is the reason the church is filled with so many people in attendance. God loves to market to the masses. Although

Sean Maddox

it is not all about mega churches alone. Mega churches do hold their weight in gold, but God performs miracles in amazing ways with small churches. God's love comes in many different forms. God's love comes from all walks of life. I do believe there will be a day in which we all worship one God. A day in which we will know the one who died for us, Jesus. God allows you to know him so that you might grow closer to him. Both God and Jesus are a major part of your resource field. Building a relationship with them will be key to your success. When you know Jesus, you know God. You know what is expected of you. No one comes to the father, except through me.

John 14:6 (King James Version)
6Jesus saith unto him, I am the way, the truth, and the life: no man cometh unto the Father, but by me.

This is the reason we pray through Jesus. Since no one comes to God, except through Jesus we must start or end our prayers "in the name of your son Jesus Christ". This shows the respect that we have for both Jesus and God for all that they have done for Christians in our lifetime. We talked about how both Jesus and God are our biggest resources that we have. Both God and Jesus are not going to run out of resources. There is plenty for everyone. We have both God and Jesus as our resource because it allows us to tap into the power that we do not hold. Both God and Jesus give us the strength that we need to complete activities, agendas, and tasks on a daily routine throughout our day. If it were not for Jesus we would not have be at the place that we are today. You might be a person that prays directly to God, which is good, but you need to learn the important of praying through Jesus Christ to hear from God. If you wonder why you are not receiving the results that you need it's because you have not given enough credit to Jesus as your Lord and savior. You have attempted to go to God without first going through Jesus. This is the reason the scripture John 14:6 says that no one comes to the father except through me.

God places people in your life so that you might have to your advantage. Life is not about using people. It's about helping one another out. Its about helping people reach their desired goals. It's about lending a hand to one another for those who need help. You might be a resource to someone else. You can help another person reach the desired goals that they need to achieve. Remember God will not give you anything that you cannot handle. God gives you more than enough. When you begin to tap into the power resource field that God has given you, you begin to know that you are on the right path. You life begins to become complete. You are in one accord with the plans that God has in store for you. Remember God does not want you to get comfortable. God wants you to continue to grow, manifest, prosper, and harvest the seeds that he has planted in your heart. He wants you to let your light shine before the world so that you might illuminate those forces of darkness. This is the way that you save lives. This is the way that you sacrifice the life that was given to you to save the life of another.

God see's that you need help, which is the reason why he places people in your distance to reach out for. God knows that it is a tough battle between the forces of good and evil which is why he has equipped you with a spiritual intelligence, which we learned about in this book in the chapter titled spiritual intelligence. This intelligence guides us towards our destiny. Its God's way of communicating with us towards the plans that he has in store for us. When you attempt to live a life on your own, you run into problems with the adversary. The adversary knows that you are away from God, which is the reason why he attacks so hard on your life. We know that the adversary is trying to sell out soul. He wants you to become a slave for him in his kingdom. This is the reason why you must keep your head in the word of God. God's word is sharper than a two edged sword. It weaves through the negativity, violence, depression, pitfalls, storms, and battles of life. The word of God holds the truth. It is pure. The word of God never lies. When you read the word you learn more about the promises that God has in store for you. The word of God is also a resources field that God has given to you as a gateway, pathway, avenue, and GPS for life. It guides you through the avenues of life. We use the word of God to rightly divide the truth. We use it so that we might know what is expected of us. The bible is the most sacred piece of literature ever written.

It holds all the answers to life. Whenever you might have a question in life, you can refer to the bible to help find your answer. Of coarse the bible will not have all the answers to your specific life questions, but it will guide you towards what is expected of you with the life that was given to you. Remember that life is a gift. It should be treated as a gift. You should take full advantage of all the resources that God has placed in your environment. God gave them to you for a reason. God gave them to you so that you will not have to go at life alone. Remember God said in Genesis 2:18 that is not good for man to be alone. God planned for man to be fruitful and multiply.

When you increase in your resources around the world you become more powerful. It enables you to do more with the life that was given to you. Ignorance is bliss. This is the reason you must continue to keep your head in the word of God and the promises that God has in store for you. The resources you have now will not be the same, as you will hold in the future. As you continue to live, you meet new people, travel new places, and try new things. You become more of complete person. You learn what is expected of you. You learn to please God. You learn to live your life for God and no one else. You cannot allow people to control your life. This is one way the adversary attempts to manipulate people. The adversary loves to control you. This is the reason you must live your life for God and not the world. The world does have much to offer, but the world is not your everything. God is your everything. God gives you the power to achieve. God gives you the power to make your dreams a reality.

Maybe you haven't lived your life for God in the past. I would love to give you chance to surrender your life to Christ. You might say, well all throughout this book you have given people more than one chance to surrender their life to Christ.

I know the importance of giving your life to Christ so that one might not sell their soul to the devil and spend an eternity in hell. I would be more than honored to give you another chance to surrender your life to Christ so that you might have eternal life in the kingdom of heaven. By reciting one of these two scriptures or even both you can save your life! You can spend an eternity in heaven knowing that you are part of the kingdom of God.

Romans 10:9 (King James Version)
9That if thou shalt confess with thy mouth the Lord Jesus, and shalt believe in thine heart that God hath raised him from the dead, thou shalt be saved.

John 3:16 (King James Version)
16For God so loved the world that he gave his only begotten Son, that whosoever believeth in him should not perish, but have everlasting life.

By saying these two very important scriptures you have saved your life and the life of others. God has given you the power to save lives. This is part of the resources that God has given you. What a powerful resource that God has given you power to save the life of ones soul! Use the resources that God has given you to save the lives of lost corrupted souls! God is a good God.

CHAPTER 16

Creativity

As a Christian believer you must learn to develop the creativity within you to advance the kingdom of God. We all have creativity within us that God has blessed us with at birth. The creativity you hold helps to define the character you hold. Creativity helps to define the person you are, you will be, and have grown to be. There are plenty of creative things you are good at that God has blessed you with. When you are creative you use your mind. You do not let your mind go to waste. You use the gifts that God has blessed you with. Creative people make things happen. They do not sit back and wait for things to happen or wait for things to come to them. God has not forgotten about you. God has a plan for your life.

When you tap into your creative power you tap into the God given ability to construct, form, and craft what's around you. You do not look at things in ordinary way. You open up your dreams. God has given you creativity to explore new avenues. You use creativity to write books, cook foods, entertain, dress, and explore. The creativity you hold is gift from Go. God has given it to you to advance the kingdom of God. You use creativity when you feel that you have no way. Where you feel there is no avenue. God allows you to use your creativity to help others. When you tap into your creative power, you tap into a gift from God. You explore new ways to make things happen. You learn to master an art form that was given to you. Your creativity is developed through your mind. This is the reason you must keep your mind sharp. You must be on the look out for the adversary who comes to kill, steal, and destroy. The adversary always attacks you in your mind, because he knows your mind is powerful. Your mind controls the creativity in which your body puts out. God has given it to you so that you might illuminate the world.

You are creative at work, at home, and at church. Other people are fascinated with the creativity that you hold. The world is filled with creative people who come together for a higher purpose to complete a mission in life. When you are creative you are vibrant. When you are creative you listen to the spirit of God. God guides you towards the plans that he has in store for you. We know that God plans are greater than our own which is the reason why we listen to the plans that God has in store for us. God's love remains the same today, tomorrow, and forever. God has given you creativity to bless others with. God wants you to use your gift to be a blessing to those people around you who need it the most.

You cannot change all people. They have to want to change themselves. They have to want to surrender their life to Christ for the plans that God has in store for them. We cannot continue to live our life to the world's standards and expect to receive the results that we want most out of life. What good is it for a man to conqueror the world and lose his soul?

Mark 8:36 (King James Version)
36For what shall it profit a man, if he shall gain the whole world, and lose his own soul?

This is the reason we store up treasures in heaven.

Matthew 6:20 (King James Version)
20But lay up for you treasures in heaven, where neither moth nor rust doth corrupt, and where thieves do not break through nor steal:

Our life on earth is temporary. It is not forever. We will soon leave this life and live a life with God eternally in heaven. This is all a part of the plans that God has in store for us.

When you don't use the gifts that God has blessed you with you are wasting talent. You are wasting the gifts that God has given you. God gave you gifts so that your light might shine in which you bless the world with. Creativity allows you to work your way through problems. It allows you to develop creative solutions to problems that occur throughout life. Creative people use their minds. They stay busy. They participate in crossword puzzles, Sudoku, scrabble, reading, and drawing. They use their mind and the talents that God has given them to realities around them. Creativity opens the door to new opportunities all around you. When you are creativity you are smart, witty, and cunning. You are clever in the sense that you outsmart the adversary. You creativity makes things possible when there is no way. You see things in people, places, and things that other people cannot see. Things that others miss. You find holes or gaps that need to be filled throughout life. You are a creative person. God needs for you to use the creativity that he has blessed you with to bless the people around you. This is part of your plan that God has in store for you. God did not give you your creativity for no reason. God needs for you to bless those around you. Maybe you are creative at cooking recipes, landscaping, fixing appliances, or good with kids. Whatever the reason may be, God needs your creativity. God did not give you this talent for no reason. God did not give you this talent to waste. You can use the talents that God has given you to bless those people around you in your environment. There are plenty of people that need blessing. There are plenty of people that need your love. You have what it takes to bless the people around you. You do not have to be superman or wonder woman to make a difference in the lives of others.

Your creativity takes you to new levels. It sets the tone for the product in which you are trying to create to make a difference in someone's life. You are a child of the highest God and you deserve the best. You cannot get down on yourself because things are not working out the way they should. All things must go according to the plans of God no matter how bad we want things to happen in our favor. God has a plan for your life and it all starts with you. It all starts with the way that you see yourself. It starts with the creativity that you have for yourself. God will not give you anything that you cannot handle. God see's the plans for your life long before you see them. When you do those things that go according to God's plans things work out in your favor.

The world is looking for people who are creative. People who can make a way when there is no way. People that hold a gift that God have given them to bless others with.

There are people in the world that need blessings from God. People that need what you have. The creativity you hold blesses people in ways that go beyond your understanding. The simple presence of your soul blesses people who do not receive the visitation that they need. You can take the time visit a patient in the hospital who does not receive visitation from the family. There are many lonely souls. You become creative to explore the gifts that God has blessed you with. You use these gifts to bless the people around you. There are many Christians and non-Christians throughout the world the need blessings. They need deliverance from the world. This is the reason millions of people are drawing closer to God. We are living in a time more Christians than ever are worshipping the Lord. There is record number of mega churches, ministries, television ministries, outreach programs, and ministers that are saving lives for the better. God is showing his love for you record setting ways. God has given you creativity to bless the people who need it the most.

Your creativity defines the way that you guide yourself. God gave you creativity to maneuver through your problems. To create avenues, answers, and solutions to your problems. Your creativity is a way to solve the problems you have in life. You create an art form of ones artistic expression. The creativity you have for yourself is very abstract. It helps to define how clever, cunning, and witty you are. The creativity that you have for yourself is a gift that is given from God. God allows you to use your talent to help the people around you achieve a level of success they have set out to achieve. Your creativity allows you to solve problems that could not be solved without a creative mind. A creative mind is a renewed mind. A transformation of ones eternal thoughts. God allows you to renew your mind to maintain your heart, mind, body, soul, and spirit.

You come together with creative forces to do the works or plans of God. God has a plan for your life and it will require you to be creative at times. It requires you to stretch and use your mind to enhance the kingdom of God through the people around you. Creative skills are acquired at an early age with kids in classes and activities such as arts and crafts. God allows your mind to become creative to stretch forth your mind. An idol mind is the devils workshop. This is why you must stay busy. The adversary will try to isolate you and keep you away from God's plans or God's best.

When you use your creativity you help to advance the kingdom of God. You help to solve creative problems that occur. When you are creative your mind does not go to waste. You use your mind and efforts to find answers to the world's problems. The foundation of our nation starts in the church. Our morals, ethics, and values are lined up with principals from God's word. We carry out the truth in God's word to advance the kingdom of God. The plans that God has in store for us are always greater than the plans that we have in store for ourselves.

Through your creativity you express yourself. You express the way that you feel towards yourself, others, and God. Your creativity is part of your personality. Its part of the genes that were given to you is birth. Your creativity describes yourself. Creativity is more than just an I.Q. When you are creative you figure out ways to find solutions to problems. You allow your mind to become active. You do not allow the enemy to box you because the creativeness you hold value is too clever to allow this to happen. You discover new life, find new ways to view life and enhance your mind muscles. Your mind becomes more active. Your mind becomes stronger. The mind is a terrible thing to waste. This is the reason why we work our mind so much. Your mind is the single most powerful asset you will not have to pay for. It's free. It doesn't cost you anything to think and the results you receive back are worth its weight in gold. Once you train your mind to do things that you want, the second you start living the life that you want to live. This is all done through creativity. Asking yourself how can I make it happen?

God gave you creativity to use as a gift. God does not want your talents to go to waste. Learn to tap into your creative. Find things that you are creative with. Find your artistic side. You might find that you have a thing for art. Your creativity is a form of art. God gave it to you as a gift to use. God wants you use your creativity to find answers to problems that occur in your life.

Learn to use the resources in your environment. Everywhere you look God has given your resources to tap into. Maybe you need a mentor, or therapist to talk to. God has placed these people in your life for a reason. These people do not always have to be professional. Sometimes an uncle or an aunt can be a mentor or person to talk or walk you through the avenues of life these people have already experienced. God places people in your life for more than one reason. God may use you to change someone's life. You may help someone find God, by taking them to church. People see you and they see the light in you. They see the creativity that you hold to make a difference in the lives of others. Remember your creativity is a gift and you should not let it go to waste. Use it to help the people around you. Use it to solve the problems in people's lives. Use it to make you stronger, become smarter, and become cleverer. The gift that God has blessed you with should be used to your advantage and the advantage of others. Wasted creativity is an unappreciation of the gift that God has given you. Continue to use your creativity to find the answers to life. Your creativities were given to you for a reason, to use to advance the kingdom of God. Use your gift to your advantage. God has given it to you for a reason. God is a good God.

CHAPTER 17

Making Your Thoughts A Reality

You have the power to make your thoughts a reality. You have the power to control your thoughts. Every thought your think is sent to the center of the universe in which the universe responds like a magnet to every thought. Your brain sends out impulses to the center of the universe with every thought that you think. The universe then responds like a magnet to the brain waves your mind sends out. The universe is like a magnet in which attracts universal signals in which that are sent out by your brain waves in which attract these thoughts in which you send out. Your mind sends out thoughts in which respond the universe responds and attracts these thoughts. Again, your mind similar to a magnet responds to the signals sent out by the universe and attracts these signals. Your mind responds to the signals sent by the universe, which enables you to have the power to control your thoughts.

The more powerful your thoughts the more power the reality in which your thoughts become a reality. You have the power to control your thoughts.

People wonder why their does good bad. For instance if you wake up in the morning and stomp your toe on the side of the bed, you respond to the cause of the effect of the situation and say darn it! Your brain sends out that negative response to the universe through a brain signal in which the universe responds to the negativity sent out through your brain. The universe then sends out signals that are also negative for your brain to respond. Your brain then responds to the negativity sent out to the universe attracting more negativity.

You then attempt to brush your teeth and spill toothpaste on your new shirt. Your brain is still responding to the negativity sent out by the universe in which you attract the same negativity. The activity continues unless you learn to control your thoughts. You must guard your mind from the negativity in which the world or the universe sends out throughout life. You have to ability to control your thoughts as you guard your mind from negativity sent out by the universe. Every thought you think can be turned into a reality. Your thoughts are a reality. They are part of who your are as person. They define you.

Your thoughts can be turned into actions or a reality. The thoughts that you think make up your character. Take the time to define what you are thinking about yourself as a person? What are you saying about yourself? How do you see yourself? What goals have you set for yourself? If you are person who has never set goals in your life and want to achieve success and have failed in the past its because you have not set any goals for your life. A person without goals is a person who set for failure. You must have plan. You must set goals for yourself. Setting goals for yourself allows God to respond to the plan that you have created with God. We continually talk about the plans that God has in store for you and it all starts with setting goals for yourself. When you set goals for yourself you layout a blueprint for the success that you want to achieve throughout life. Your goals are part of your thoughts. Every goal you set is thought that is arranging or setting up a good karma for the universe to respond. Instead of having negative karma from negative thoughts attracted to you now have the power to control your thoughts in which you send out to the universe.

Start by setting good goals for yourself. Make a plan. Make a list of or plan of where you want to see yourself in five years. What do you want to achieve? What do you want to accomplish?

Make a list of this criteria and how you plan to reach these goals. You now are thinking positive thoughts. You now are setting up or arranging a good karma is your favor. The universe is ready to respond to the signal or brain waves being sent out to the universe.

You wonder why your days have been going so bad, its because you haven't yet mastered the faith of controlling your thoughts. You haven't taken the time to discipline yourself to the power you hold to controlling or taming your thoughts. You have the ability to control things in your life. You have the ability of making your thoughts a reality. You can attract the things that you want out of life and it all starts with you. It all starts with taming your thoughts. You have the power to control your thoughts. God has given you the power. As a Christian believer you do not have to live in defeat. You do not have to live in poverty. The same as wealth, poverty is a state of mind. It's the way you view yourself. It's the plans that you have for your future. You do not have to live in poverty or defeat. You have the power to overcome. Every setback is a setup for your comeback.

When you learn to control your thoughts, you learn to master your thoughts. You discover what your thoughts are. You discover what your thoughts will become. You learn a lot about yourself in the way that you view yourself. The way that you view your future. Remember your thoughts are your reality. Why wouldn't you want to control your thoughts, your reality, your future, and your destiny? You have the power to control.

You may wonder why you go out to different locations or destinations and see friends of family on spur of the moment occasions. You have thought about these individuals before in which your sent out those signals to the universe and the universe responds. The universe does take time to respond. Occurrences can take up to days, weeks, months or even years to occur. Do not get discouraged if you are not making instant results. Your thoughts will soon become a reality to your life. The universe will respond.

You define yourself by the thoughts that you think. Your thoughts say a lot about the person you are, the person you will grow to be, and the person you are soon to become.

You have to learn to develop your state of mind. Your state of mind is like a vault in holds the prized value of your conscious. Your conscious is the reality your create with the impulse of every thought. This is the science of your thinking. You can break down your thoughts through mental meditation or mind therapy. You now write down your thoughts tracking the power of each thought. You have the power of tracking each and every thought and praying over thoughts in which you want to exit your mind. Do not welcome thoughts in which you do not feel comfortable with. Control your destiny. Control who you are as person. Control what others are saying about you, but most importantly what you are saying about yourself. Be the one in control. Learn self-control and what it means to master your thoughts. What it means to control thoughts that are not wanted. Controlling the thoughts in which your choose to meditate on. Thoughts that make you happy. Thoughts that make you love. Thoughts that make you feel loved. You have the power to control your destiny. You have the power to control that you are as a person. You have the power to set your life down the right path. When you are one with God you are in alignment and the harmony that God has for your life. God allows you to control your life. God allows you to control the person that you are. You have the power to control your destiny.

This is why the adversary fights you so hard in your thoughts. The adversary knows the power of your thoughts. The adversary knows that if he can control your thoughts, he can control you. This is why God has given you the power to control your thoughts. Your thoughts make up important aspects in your life. They help to guide your life. This is why people with scattered thoughts live such scattered lives. You must learn to control your thoughts to live a controlled life. You are child of the highest God. You make your thoughts a reality. Your thoughts are your destiny. They define who you are as a person.

Sean Maddox

When you learn to control your thoughts you enable yourself to control that you are as a person. We know that your thoughts are your character. They help to make up your demeanor.

Answers.com reported that as of 2001, the top 1% of households the upper class owned 33.4% of all privately held wealth, and the next 19% (the managerial, professional, and small business stratum) had 51%, which means that just 20% of the people owned a remarkable 84%, leaving only 16% of the wealth for the bottom 80% (wage and salary workers. These people have learned to control their thoughts. They have learned to control the signals in which they are putting out into the universe. They know how to get the universe to respond to the thoughts they are putting out. Taking time to master your thoughts takes self-control and discipline. You have the power to attract wealth, happiness, family, friends, relationships, love, and abundance.

Learn to control your thoughts and you can learn to build your state of mind. You can learn to control how powerful your thoughts are. How many times of day your meditate on one thought. Who you discuss your thoughts with?

This is why it's important to discuss your thoughts. Having a mentor in your life helps. Mint ors help to guide your life. They help you avoid pitfalls. There are many avenues, situations, and problems that mentors have been through in which they can share their input to the many problems they have encountered in life. Being a mentor to someone in your life is act of Christian faith. You learn to combine or collaborate your ideas or thoughts with others to accomplish goals or achieve success. When you are together with a team you are more powerful. You enable yourself to do more, get more accomplished. You work together as a team to build thoughts that become a reality. This is better accomplished with careful planning of your thoughts. You build thoughts as you share ideas with others about the goals that you set out to accomplish. Any person with goals is set for failure. You achieve more when you write out your goals, ideas, dreams, and aspirations. Begin to arrange a good karma for yourself by writing out your goals on paper. Write ideas that you plan to accomplish. Ideas that you plan to better yourself. This is why successful people are successful because they have a plan. It is not harder to lose. They have allowed themselves to coach themselves. Self-education is one of the greatest educations known to man. You learn real life scenarios through education yourself or learning on your own. You learn to master life and all life has to offer. Do not be afraid of your thoughts. The adversary attempts to instill fear in you to keep you away from the plans that God has in store for you. Control the signals the universe sends out and responds to be controlling your thoughts. You have the power to control your thoughts. God is a good God.

CHAPTER 18

Sacrifice

A sacrifice is defined as the surrender or destruction of something prized or desirable for the sake of something considered as having a higher or more pressing claim. As a Christian believer, you must learn to sacrifice. Many aspects come into effect throughout the kingdom of criteria that must be sacrificed. You sacrifice what you have on the line. What it counts for and what you stand for. We all stand for something. Something that we believe in you. Something that we set out to accomplish. It is the American way. What is it that you stand for? What is it that you believe? What do you set out to achieve and how will you achieve it? Through sacrifice. You sacrifice everything that you stand for you. Everything that you believe. It's that you believe that defines you. It reveals the morals and ethics that you have for yourself. In what was are you disciplined? In what ways do you obey God?

Jesus was a living sacrifice to us. Jesus' blood was shed on the cross for our sins, so that we might be saved having eternal life in the kingdom of heaven. Jesus sacrificed. Jesus sacrificed his life for you. This is the appreciate Jesus had for God. This shows how Jesus was obedient to Christ because both Jesus and God loved you. Jesus loved you enough to give his life to save the world from sin. There is nothing to adversary can do.

You have been set apart from the world called out on a mission through Christ. A mission from God in which you will complete in or to complete the kingdom of God.

Ephesians 1:4 (King James Version)
According as he hath chosen us in him before the foundation of the world, that we should be holy and without blame before him in love:

God calls us out before the foundation of the world to complete a mission in life. In this way we are sacrificing the life given to us through God to complete a mission in which we will receive eternal life in heaven. When God called us out before the foundation of the world, he planted a seed in us. A seed that is incorruptible. This is seed cannot be broken. God knew you when he created you. He knew your every thought, your every action, your every plan, and your destiny. God knew the plans that he had in store for you long before he created you. It is all-apart of the plan that God has in store for you. As a sacrifice to the kingdom of God, God's plan will work. God will complete the work in which he has begun in you. God loves you more than you can imagine

God is still developing you into a mold. God is molding with everyday that goes by. God is configuring you into his creation, his masterpiece. God loves for you will remain the same through his creation until his plans are down.

God plan for you requires you to save souls. God planned for you to win over souls. Souls that have lost, corrupted, and sold, sold to the devil. The devil wants your soul. The devil wants to keep you away from the plans that God has in store for you. Since God plans consist of you saving souls, God allows us to win over the souls of Christians. There are two important scriptures in the bible that allow you to save the life of a Christian. These scriptures were written as past of Gods plan for you. The scriptures John 3:16 and Romans 10:9 allow you to save the soul of a Christian.

Sean Maddox

John 3:16 (King James Version)
16For God so loved the world that he gave his only begotten Son, that whosoever believeth in him should not perish, but have everlasting life.

Romans 10:9 (King James Version)
9That if thou shalt confess with thy mouth the Lord Jesus, and shalt believe in thine heart that God hath raised him from the dead, thou shalt be saved.

You have the power to win over souls. You have the power to control your destiny and allow a Christian to reach heaven. In heaven life is eternal. Life is forever. There is no crime, murder, violence, abortions, and theft, kidnapping, robbing, or lying. Heaven is a perfect place. A place of no sin. A place you can call him and will call home. This is all possible through the sacrifice of your life. Committing and surrounding your life to Christ. Sacrifice is such a power action. God has the ability to move mountains. The sacrifice of your life is the one that consist of the plans that God has in store for you.

Many people sacrifice their lives to Christ. They have come to the realization that this is the plan that God has in store for you. The reason this book was written is because billions of people throughout the world from all different walks of life come to Christ at different times in their life. Some early, some later. No matter what time of your life you came to Christ you are a late bloomer. You may feel it has taken to long, but you are a late bloomer. You bloom at a time that is convent to Christ. You bloom at a time that go according to Gods plan for you. A flower is such a precious gift. You are a precious gift to God that is why you are a late bloomer. You are a masterpiece creation to God.

Many people get worried about the things that they have done in life. They worry about their past, what they have done wrong and what they should have done better. The adversary, the enemy always likes to fight you in your past. He loves to bring up the past negative situations in your life to remind that you are not good enough to reach the level of success that you have set out to reach. The adversary is clever and cunning. Cunning in the sense that he outwits his opponents. He outsmarts them. The adversary is both book smart and street smart. He had mastered the art of literature and mastered the art of the streets. He comes in all different shapes and sizes. The adversary same plan is to sacrifice your life. The adversary wants to sell your soul, so that you may be a slave to him in his kingdom, which will be earth. This is the reason the adversary is so clever. As you become smarter and smarter as the days go by so does the adversary. The adversary works hard to win your soul. This is why he attempts to get you to sin so much. The adversary is trying to trap you. He is trying to keep you away from the plans that God has in store for you.

Romans 12:2 (King James Version)
2And be not conformed to this world: but be ye transformed by the renewing of your mind, that ye may prove what is that good, and acceptable, and perfect, will of God.

This is the reason we are not of this world. Remember we were put here temporarily for a mission. To save lives. Remember you have the power to save lives through Romans 10:9 and John 3:16. This is part of the plan that God has in store for you. You have always wondering why do exist? What is the plan or purpose that God has in store for you? God needs for you to win over lives! You hold the power to save lives.

John 18:36 (King James Version)
36Jesus answered, My kingdom is not of this world: if my kingdom were of this world, then would my servants fight, that I should not be delivered to the Jews: but now is my kingdom not from hence.

This is the reason God says that we are in this world, but not of this world. Earth will eventually belong to Satan. Our eternal life is in heaven, which is where we will go after we leave earth. God will destroy this world with fire. The first world was destroyed through a massive flood that God saved Noah family. This is why God instructed Noah to build an ark. He instructed Noah to board one mal and one female of every living creator on the face of the earth.

God sacrificed. God has been sacrificing his whole life. His creation consists of billions of sacrifices.

Genesis 6

1And it came to pass, when men began to multiply on the face of the earth, and daughters were born unto them,

2That the sons of God saw the daughters of men that they were fair; and they took them wives of all, which they chose.

3And the LORD said, my spirit should not always strive with man, for that he also is flesh: yet his days shall be an hundred and twenty years.

4There were giants in the earth in those days; and also after that, when the sons of God came in unto the daughters of men, and they bare children to them, the same became mighty men, which were of old, men of renown.

5And God saw that the wickedness of man was great in the earth, and that every imagination of the thoughts of his heart was only evil continually.

6And it repented the LORD that he had made man on the earth, and it grieved him at his heart.

7And the LORD said, I will destroy man whom I have created from the face of the earth; both man, and beast, and the creeping thing, and the fowls of the air; for it repented me that I have made them.

8But Noah found grace in the eyes of the LORD.

9These are the generations of Noah: Noah was a just man and perfect in his generations, and Noah walked with God.

10And Noah begat three sons, Shem, Ham, and Japheth.

11The earth also was corrupt before God, and the earth was filled with violence.

12And God looked upon the earth, and, behold, it was corrupt; for all flesh had corrupted his way upon the earth.

13And God said unto Noah, The end of all flesh is come before me; for the earth is filled with violence through them; and, behold, I will destroy them with the earth.

14Make thee an ark of gopher wood; rooms shalt thou make in the ark, and shalt pitch it within and without with pitch.

15And this is the fashion, which thou shalt make it of: The length of the ark shall be three hundred cubits, the breadth of it fifty cubits, and the height of it thirty cubits.

16A window shalt thou make to the ark, and in a cubit shalt thou finish it above; and the door of the ark shalt thou set in the side thereof; with lower, second, and third stories shalt thou make it.

17And, behold, I, even I, do bring a flood of waters upon the earth, to destroy all flesh, wherein is the breath of life, from under heaven; and every thing that is in the earth shall die.

18But with thee will I establish my covenant; and thou shalt come into the ark, thou, and thy sons, and thy wife, and thy sons' wives with thee.

19And of every living thing of all flesh, two of every sort shalt thou bring into the ark, to keep them alive with thee; they shall be male and female.

20Of fowls after their kind, and of cattle after their kind, of every creeping thing of the earth after his kind, two of every sort shall come unto thee, to keep them alive.

21And take thou unto thee of all food that is eaten, and thou shalt gather it to thee; and it shall be for food for thee, and for them.

22Thus did Noah; according to all that God commanded him, so did he.

This is how angry Noah was

This is how angry God was with the world that the world lived in disobedience. In the same way that God had destroyed the first world, God will destroy the second world. It is past of the plan that God has in store for us. This is why you God needs for you to save lives. We are sacrificing out lives for God. God is a good God.

CHAPTER 19

Downfall

The devil wants to see you fail and fall. This is all apart of the downfall. As a Christian believer if you have fallen, you have to get back up, dust yourself off, and find yourself again. We all get off track in life from time to time. Its part of the life cycle of life that evolves through a natural sense of human fatigue. During your downfall and it will come you have to find your hustlers spirit.

The adversary try's to attack your home, family, life, spirit, and finances. The adversary attempts to attack me all the time with writers block, but I know that the talent that comes from within is God given. The same talent that you hold that is God given that will help you make the most of your life. You are talented beyond measure. You are special to God. Let your talents show. You have talents that you have not released yet. God plans work out according to his plans at a given time. The plans that you have may not work out according to your plans, but they work out according to God's plans. We all go through struggles in life from time to time. Its part of the evolution of life.

This is when you have to learn to be creative with the talents that God has given you. Your creativity will help to define you, your life, and the gifts that God has given you. The same as your hustler's spirit, your creative comes from within. In the modern days that we live in you have to learn to be creative. You have to learn what sets you apart from your competition and believe me there will be plenty of competition as you compete in life. God moves you towards the direction or that plans that he has in store for you, as you grow closer to him. God leads you to direction or plans that God has in store for you. It never always works out the way that you want to work out. You have hidden talents inside of you that have not been released.

Sure you may be a nobody now, but you will not always be that way. If you look at anyone that has ever made it, they were once a nobody. They started in the same place that you started. They had to work hard, hustle, and keep a positive mind in the most severe situations. The adversary is always trying to figure you out. The adversary is always trying to keep you away from the plans that God has in store for you. The adversary deceives you! The adversary try's to convince you that his ways are the best ways. He will attempt to show you all that he has to offer you if you give him your soul! The adversary wants your soul and he will stop at nothing to get it and he will get it if you allow him. You have something to offer the world that God has created in you. You may feel as though you do not know God, which may be very much true. God is ready to build a relationship with you. You may be distant from God in your past, but it doesn't always have to be this way. You may thing, well what if I am not good enough. You simply have to be yourself! Being yourself pays off in ways that go beyond your imagination. People can relate to you when you are yourself. People see that truth in you and relate. No one can relate to someone who is not real. Why would you want to be someone or something that your not? First off, your uncomfortable attempting to be someone that your not. You spend your whole time focused on someone or something that your not. You're not being your real self.

God forgives you for the sins that you have committed. Sure you have committed sins in your life. People have lied, cheated, stole, cheated on husbands or wives and committed sins that ate right into the adversary hands. Sins so bad that you have sat up at night crying. Believe me, I feel you pain! God feels your pain! God created, so God knows you. God has not forgotten about you! Continue to do the things that God has put you on this earth to do

There will be times when you are not feeling it.

Show God that he has created a good work in you. Show God what you were put on this earth for. You have plenty to offer the world. You have plenty to take from the world the God has laid out for you to have. The world has so much to offer in which you will receive much from. You have to know that you have been created in the likeness of God, the creator of heaven and earth.

Know that your downfall will come in the same realm as your failure, which is part of your success. Do not have to accept failure. Accept the position that you are in and know that you are a child of the highest God. Your downfall along with the adversary attempts to keep you away from the plans that God has in store for you. Your downfall attempts to hold you at a stand still. A point in life in which you feel that you cannot go on. A point in life that takes a hold of you attempting to drain you from the very promises that God has in store for you. As a Christian believer, you have to be able to keep a positive head. You have to know that God has something greater in store for you. During your downfall people will try to manipulate your life. People will try to control you. Try to tell you what to do. Tell you that you are not good enough or that you do not have what it takes. God says different. God has created you in the likeness of him. You might have achieved the level of success that you want, but your breakthrough is right around the corner. You have been equipped with everything that you need to succeed. God has made you in the likeness of him. You cannot focus on the pits, the storms, and the downfalls of life. Downfalls will come. This is part of life. Failure will come. Failure will happen throughout life. Remember its part of the evolution of life. As a Christian believer, focus on the plans that God has in store for you. Remember to lean not until thy own understanding.

Proverbs 3:5 (King James Version)
5 Trust in the LORD with all thane heart; and lean not unto thane own understanding.

When you lean not until your own understanding, you are saying that you trusting God with your life. Your trusting that God has the plans in store for you that will allow you to reach the level of success that you have set out to achieve. God has great things in store for you when you believe this with all your heart. You have not been put on this earth for no reason. God has called you out before the foundation of the world.

Ephesians 1:4 (King James Version)
4 According as he hath chosen us in him before the foundation of the world, that we should be holy and without blame before him in love:

God has set you apart from the world. You are of this world, but you are not in this world.

Romans 12:2 (King James Version)
2 And be not conformed to this world: but be ye transformed by the renewing of your mind, that ye may prove what is that good, and acceptable, and perfect, will of God.

I have written this book to help you with your walk with the Lord. God will bring you to a point in life that allows you to realize that you cannot make it without God. You cannot live in this world alone. The adversary loves isolation, which is why he attempts to keep you away from the kingdom of God. The world is hungry for Gods love. Millions of people throughout the world are searching to know more about the plans that God has in store for them. Millions of people throughout the world are searching for the love that God has in store for them.

You may feel as though you have been distant from God. God is searching to build a lasting relationship with you. As a

Christian believer, you build a lasting relationship with God through searching the scriptures throughout the bible. God has laid out blueprint for success for those who decided to receive the love that God has in store for them. God has given you all that you need to succeed. God has laid out the blueprint for you. This is the love that God has for you in which God needs for you to succeed. God did not plan for you to stay stuck in the same position your whole life. God has plan for your life when you believe. You have to train your mind to listen to the still small voice. God speaks to you everyday; often times we are too busy to take the time to even notice God speaking. We often caught up in the troubles of the world in what that brings that we miss the opportunities of advance for the forward production of the kingdom of God in which what God has in store for us. God will come to you during your downfall to speak to you the plans that God has in store for you.

The adversary wants you to stay stuck in a rut in which you cannot see the many plans that God has in store for you. The adversary attempts to blind you in which you cannot see a clear path to your success. The adversary knows that God has great things in store for you in will try everything in his power to keep you away from the plans that God has in store for you. You have to believe that God has something great in store for you. The problem with most people is that they stop believing. The adversary comes into their life and they start believing the things of this world rather than believe God. You cannot believe what man says about you, you have to believe what God is telling you. God is looking to grow a relationship with you everyday.

Many times we come to our downfall in order to grow closer to God. God will take his hand of favor off of you to allow certain things to happen to you that will allow you to grow closer to him. When you are off track with God, God is attempting to draw you closer to him. When you are off track with God your life comes to a dead end. Your life comes to a halt. It stops and its stops for a reason. God is preparing to do a great work within you and the people around you. Do not stop going to church. Do not stop inviting your friends and family to church. To many times we stop the plans that God has in store for us when we are closet to our breakthrough. This is when the adversary will fight you his hardest.

You may feel as though you do not know enough about God. You know that God loves you and that is what counts. God loves you enough to give his only son that died on the cross for you. Jesus blood was shed on the cross for your sins. This is the love that God has for you. It's amazing to know that Jesus died for the sins that you commit. Every sin in which you have committed has been taken care of. This is the love that God has for you. It's part of the plan that God has in store for you. You area victor and not the victim. You have been called out before the foundation of the world to be an ambassador for Christ.

You have plenty to offer the world through God. You know plenty about the word of God. God has equipped you with all that you need. God will finish a work in you that will allow one to go to heaven to receive eternal life.

Remember that your downfall is a sign that your breakthrough is right around the corner. You are child of the highest God. God is a good God.

CHAPTER 20

An Empty Heart

Imagine you lost the life of a loved one. Someone in which you knew. Something you grew to know. I best friend. An advisor. A companion. Someone you loved with a passion. Someone you cherish. God brings those special people in our lives for a reason. These people help us to get through our life. They help us with projects, with relationships, love, lust, passion, and work. God brings the people you need along your path to complete a mission in life. God will bring someone along your path to help you get over the lost of a loved one. Maybe you have had a boyfriend or girlfriend that came into your life that provided the extra love that you need. The extra companion you have been looking for, for years. God knows what you need in life. God knows the love, joy, passion, happiness, and laughter that your heart, mind, body, soul, and spirit have been aching for. We all have had an empty heart at times. Something that we have been longing for. Something our body pays attention to, but our heart has not yet responded. We don't know why our mind doesn't do what our heart tells it to do. As Christians, we must be smart in life. We must make smart decisions towards the direction in which our life is headed. God places people in your life to get over certain situations we cannot come through on our own. These people provide the extra love that we need on rainy days.

The adversary tries to take our hearts away. The adversary tries to take away the very love that our heart needs to function throughout our life. Your heart is one of the most important organs in the human body. It is responsible for pumping your blood through your blood vessels to different organs, body parts, and functions of the bible. Your heart is like a generator for your body which pumps blood to the given vessels. You may have someone in your life that has helped you get through a situation like the lost have loved one. You cannot go through life alone and expect to receive the best that God has to off. The adversary likes isolation. He loves to get you alone to which you are now in a vulnerable state of mind. He knows that if he can keep you away from God, he can keep you from hearing from God. This is a quick way the adversary can allow your heart to become empty. While in isolation or an empty state of mind you begin to miss your loved ones. You begin to miss the medicine your body needs to heal itself. Your body becomes depressed. You remain in isolation isolated away from the people you need the most. Since you are distant from the light the you become immune to the darkness in which you think it is okay. This is a trap from the devil. This is the way the devil attempts to lure you in. The allure of the situation is too bright to the eye. This is the wrong light. This is the light the adversary attempts to reveal to you is the way. This is the life the adversary wants you to live. The adversary is attempting to sell your soul in which you become a slave to him. We know that adversary comes to kill, steal, and destroy throughout the world. The adversary's main goal is to sell your soul, which is why he works so hard to keep you away from the plans that God has in store for you.

Your heart was created to orchestrate. It was created to command or give orders. Your heart is a leader, not a follower. Your heart leads the way for your blood in your body. The same as your heart must lead your mind, soul, body, and spirit. Your heart follows what your mind tells it. Your mind tells your heart what to do. This is the reason we must guard our minds from the evilness of the world. God made your heart to be tenderhearted forgiving one another.

Ephesians 4:32 (King James Version)
32And are ye kind one to another, tenderhearted, forgiving one another, even as God for Christ's sake hath forgiven you.

God needs for you to forgive those people around you that have done you wrong. When you do not forgive you allow corruption to fill your heart. A darkness, which is a dark spirit from the adversary, comes into your heart, mind, body, soul, and spirit and eats at your soul. The corruption attempts to shutdown the commandments of your heart, which allow your body to function. This alters the very plans that God has in store for you.

The adversary loves to attack our families. Our families are closet to our hearts. This is the very reason the adversary is after your family. The adversary tries to make you sacrifice your life or the life of another, which is the result of a sold soul to the devil. When your soul is sold your life becomes the adversaries forever. This is why God offered his sons life for the life of ours. The adversary knows how important your heart is. This is the reason we must guard our hearts. We must leave our hearts protected from the evilness of the adversary. Your heart is filled with love for all. Your heart leads the way for your mind, body, soul, and spirit to follow. As you guard your heart you guard the direction of which your life is headed. God gives the plan for your life, which is closest to your heart. God knows you heart. He knows where your heart is. He knows where your feelings are. God answers prayers towards people have been faithful to him. People that have been honest to his principals.

The result of an empty heart could be the reason for you blooming late in life. Your empty heart could have lead to an obstacle in which you has attempted to keep you away from the plans that God has in store for you life. You may have lost a loved one. Or your husband or wife has left you. This hurts our hearts, because these people are closest to our hearts. You have feeling the same as anyone else. God knows your feelings. God see's your pain. God is here providing the comfort that you need for your pain. You do not have to go around in misery or defeat. God has a comeback for your setback. You now live in victory not defeat. God says he will never leave you nor forsake you. You have to believe that with all of your heart, mind, body, soul, and spirit. This is why we must guard our hearts. We must guard what we are listening to. Guard what we are hearing. God what we are seeing. The adversary would love to fill your mind with jargon that is not good for soul.

There are many of you with empty hearts. Many of you that have lost the life of a loved one. Someone you really cared for. Someone you really knew. Someone that had that lasting impression on you. A person you kicked it with, hung out with, or passed the time by. God brought that person in your life to make your heart stronger for what next he has in store for you. God brought the person in your life to help you get through your next stages of life. There will come a time that you will see that person again. A time in which you will reunite. For now, God needs for you complete the work that has been given you to complete your mission in life. God needs for you save the souls of those people around you. People who are lost. People who have no direction. People who need help in which they have lost God. DO not listen to the ways of the adversary. It is by no accident that you are reading this book. This book is part of your destiny. Its part of your future. Its part of where you are headed in life. That book has been written to save your life. This book has been written to give you eternal life in heaven for the day that Jesus returns for you. This is the love that God has for you. God loves you more than you can imagine. God will not give you more than you can handle which is the reason he has given you a mission or purpose in life. Remember this book is written to save lives and help you to save the lives of Christians you witness to as part of your mission below. Listed below are three scriptures that save the life of Christian believer when they believe that Jesus died on the cross for their sins so that they may have eternal life.

John 3:16 (King James Version)
16For God so loved the world that he gave his only begotten Son, that whosoever believeth in him should not perish, but have everlasting life.

Romans 10:9 (King James Version)
9That if thou shalt confess with thy mouth the Lord Jesus, and shalt believe in thine heart that God hath raised him from the dead, thou shalt be saved.

We have listed these scriptures throughout this book to help save the life of believer. The importance of a saved soul is too close to God's heart. God wants you to draw close to him. It is important that you keep a pure heart. When you have a pure heart with God you have a pure mind, body, soul, and spirit. You can hear from God. You are not worried about the ways of the world in what it might do to you because you are in the hands of all mighty God. God brings you out of a peak, valley, pits, storm, and battle. God will deliver you through what it is you are going through. God allows us to go through things to grow closer to him, but to ultimately become stronger in the process. There is nothing our God cannot handle. Nothing is too big for him.

If there is someone who has done you wrong, you need to learn to have forgiveness in your heart. This is the reason God allows you to forgive those people around you in your environment. Many people do people wrong because they don't know no better or out of evilness of their heart. Whatever the reason may be God is here for you. God is here to provide the light that you need to guide you. When you know your heart, you know yourself. You know what you are capable of. You know what God ask of you, his plans, and what he has in store for you. God will not do anything to hurt you. God will never leave you nor forsake you.

Your heart, mind, body, soul, and spirit are full of light. Which is the reason God wants you heart to shine for all people to see. God wants you to illuminate the world so that they might see the love that he has for them.

Matthew 5:16 (King James Version)
16Let you're light so shine before men, that they may see your good works, and glorify your Father which is in heaven.

God allows you light to shine before the world so that they may see the path that God has in store for them. Your light belongs to the kingdom of God. It guides people to the promises that God has in store for them. God has a plan for your life. The reason your life has not come out the way that it should in the past is because you have attempted to live your life without a plan. You have attempted to live your life for everyone else, but yourself. You cannot go around worrying about other people's problems throughout your life. Others peoples problems are their problems. That's between them and God. You have your own problems to worry about. They're no problem to big for our God. There is no problem that our God cannot handle. God delivers you through the storms of life at his time. Nothing ever goes according to plans of us. We are on God's time.

We talked earlier in the chapter about leaders and followers. Leaders are peopling the support one another. Maybe you are not leader. Maybe you are more of what a supporting actor would be. Supporting actor supports the lead role. He supports the star. Many of us think we are leaders, but we play a better supporting role. Let me let you in on a little secret. All lead role people were once supporting actors for someone. You have to learn how to support before you can lead. Supporting someone is an act of leading. You are a leader at heart. I could tell you in my life, my job decryption is much more of a supporting actor type of role. Look at someone like Matt Damon. Matt Damon is both a supporting actor type of person and lead role person. Look at the move Oceans, Eleven, Twelve, and Thirteen. Matt

Doman alongside actors such as George Clooney, Brad Pitt, Matt Damon, Catherine Zeta Jones, Andy Garcia, Don Chile, Bernice Mac, and Julia Roberts. Matt Damon supported these actors. He wasn't needed for a lead role. He wasn't need for more than what he was created for. God used him exactly for what he was created for. God does not always need us to play a leading role. You can still be a star and not play the leading role. You have to know yourself and know your position and play it will. God needs for you to play your role well. In the movie Bourne Supremacy, Matt plays as the leading role as a framed for a botched CIA operation he is forced to take up his former life as a trained assassin to survive. Matt is still a star a supporting role or a leading role. You are a child of the highest God. God loves you more than you can imagine. God has great things in store for you. God is a good God,

CHAPTER 21

Seasons

Ecclesiastes 3
1 There is a time for everything, and a season for every activity under the heavens:

Seasons bring change. They allow one to mold and develop in the person that God created you to be. You may be discouraged that you dreams, goals, and aspirations have not come to past yet. This is because your dreams must come to past in their due season.

Leviticus 26:4 (King James Version)
4Then I will give you rain in due season, and the land shall yield her increase, and the trees of the field shall yield their fruit.

This is a promise from God that the land shall increase. God says that you will eat the good of the land.

Isaiah 1:19 (King James Version)
19If ye be willing and obedient, ye shall eat the good of the land:

God promises that our will eat the good of the land. When you are willing and obedient to God, God blesses you. You must obey the commands of God. You must be willing to listen to God as he instructs you. If you are careful to not give up, you will see your plans come to past.

Galatians 6:9 (King James Version)
9And let us not be weary in well doing: for in due season we shall reap, if we faint not.

Your plans will not always work out the way that you want them to. They will not always work out when you want them to. They must work out according to the plans of God in his due season. Plans happen at specific times for specific reasons because they are the plans of God's and not yours. God's plans are always greater than your own throughout life. You cannot rush the plans that God has in store for you. They must happen in their due season.

Each season throughout life brings value to the kingdom of God. Some seasons are abundant seasons, some seasons are dry seasons. Whatever the reason might be, it works out according to the plans that God has in store for the kingdom of God. You develop your character through each season that you encounter. Season bring happy times. Times of joy, peace, happiness, and laughter. The season allows you to take all of your cares into one bundle and allows one to set out to accomplish ones dreams.

Seasons for praying are seasons for planting seeds. You may go through a season of praying in which you lift up all of your needs to the Lord thy God. You communicate one on one with God towards the living testimonies and real life situations that occur throughout your life. We learned that we sacrificed our life be surrendering our life to Christ. This all happened in a season. A season that was planned by God. Your season of praying allows you to form your life together. It allows you to vent out all of your problems and frustrations to God that are occurring in your life. We all go through problems in life. Some greater than others. Whatever your problem may be, God is there for you every step of the way. You do not have to go through your problems alone. God is here to answer your prayers.

We go through seasons in which are prayers are answered. God here's your prayer. He here's the problem that you are going through. You do not have to go at your problems alone. You have God to vent your issues to. God needs for you to come to him every step of the way. We know that when two people come together in agreement with God our prayers are answered.

When you pray you are planting seeds. The same as the incorruptible seed that was planted in us when you were given eternal life those same seeds are panted in prayer to God. These seeds cannot be broken. They are part of an incorruptible seed that cannot be broken.

God needs for you to come to him in prayer. God already knows you needs. God knows every hair on your head. What an amazing thought. God is looking to build a relationship with you. God is looking to know you better. He looks to build a lasting relationship with you. Some seasons take longer than others. Some seasons are meant for change. They are meant to transform a non-believer into a believer. There are millions of non-believer that need saving. Non-believer that has lost corrupted souls. Souls that have strayed off coarse for the plans that God has in store for them. This is why these people experience their lost for a season.

Psalm 145:15 (King James Version)
15The eyes of all wait upon thee; and thou gives them their meat in due season.

God promises to bless you in your due season. The reason plant seeds are to reap abundance in harvest. God has a harvest for you. God has a plan for your life that allows you to receive eternal life throughout he kingdom of heaven. When you are one with God you listen to the plans that God has in store for you. You are obedient to Christ is which you will receive an abundance in harvest.

You have to plan for the season ahead. The same as you check the weather channel to view the weather in your local town to prepare for a day in its due season, you prepare for a season that God has in store for you. Seasons bring you change, they bring blessings, abundance, and peace. There is a peace that comes upon God when you are in your due season. God needs for you bless the people around you. This is why some people only come into your life for a season. Some come into your life for a lifetime. The people that come into your life for a season are placed in your life to accomplish a certain goal, task, or objective planned by God. Things happen in a due season for a reason. It goes according to the plans that God has in store for you. Everything must come into alignment and harmony with God.

Seasons bring forth the change that you need. Change in family, change in business, change in relationships and change in finances. Your changes occur according to the growth the occurs throughout your life. You are continually growing. God is raises you to new levels. God never wants you to get stuck in a rut or comfortable with your current situation. God wants you to continue to grow and prosper. This is part of the plans that God has in store for you. God is ready to perform miracles in your life. Your life is in need of change. When you get stuck in a rut throughout life you do not grow. Things around you become dead which is unhealthy for the kingdom of God. That is never a good look.

God brings the people that you need in your life to stir up joy, peace, and abundance in your life. This is why people with tons of energy come around you. God see's that you are tired in life, so he brings people with a high energy field in your life to keep you moving towards the plans that God has in store for you. When you listen to God all things will line up in your favor. The plans that God has in store for you will come to past. You begin to live your life, as a true Christian knows your faith. You will know your destiny because you know the plans that God has in store for you. You know the plans that God has in store for you because you have built a relationship with God. God is looking to speak to you on daily basis. God loves you more than you can imagine. This is why you must continue to build a relationship with God daily.

God wants you to grow with him through the season. God does not want it all to happen fast at once. God wants to slowly build you to the level of success that he wants to see you achieve throughout the world.

You must learn to be patient. Everything will not occur as fast as you want it to happen. We know that it must happen in its due season. It must occur when God wants it to happen. This is why we are patient with God in the plans that he has in store for us. Too many people throughout the world are living their life to the worlds. When God created the world he did it in seasons. It did not all happen at once.

Genesis 1

1In the beginning God created the heaven and the earth.

2And the earth was without form, and void; and darkness was upon the face of the deep. And the Spirit of God moved upon standards. We are not of this world. We were put in this world temporarily for mission or purpose to complete through Christ.

When God created the world he created the face of the waters.

3And God said, Let there be light: and there was light.

4And God saw the light, that it was good: and God divided the light from the darkness.

5And God called the light Day, and the darkness he called Night. And the evening and the morning were the first day.

6And God said, Let there be a firmament in the midst of the waters, and let it divide the waters from the waters.

7And God made the firmament, and divided the waters, which were under the firmament from the waters, which were above the firmament: and it was so.

8And God called the firmament Heaven. And the evening and the morning were the second day.

God did all this in season. It was his appointed season. Everything in life happens in its due season. God is good God.

CHAPTER 22

Wealth

You hold the power to get wealth. The wealth you have from within you is given to you at birth. Wealth is held within you genes. Wealth is the person you are. It's a state of mind. It's the way you view yourself. Wealth is a state of mind of a description of currency that exists throughout the world. The power to get wealth is held responsibly up to you.

The adversary attempts to put a curse on your ability to get wealth. The adversary simply does not want you to make it in means of wealth. Wealth is what you acquire in the form of a currency. It is more than a bank statement. It is more than a deposit or withdrawal. It is more than a vault in the Cayman Islands filled with money. Wealth defines what you have acquired materialistically. What you have gained from the world. Wealth says a lot about your values, what you stand for, and how you look to define yourself throughout life. You get money through acquiring, developing, and building a state of mind. A state of mind that acts as a platform that operates the functions of your character. Your character is defined by the way you are. The way you view yourself, the love that you have for yourself and the love that you have for others. You cannot buy your way to heaven. Heaven is given to those who are saved and believe that Jesus died for their sins. Heaven is where you will find true wealth. Wealth is the means of acquiring money in abundance. It's the amount of money you can live on before going broke. This is the reason so many people try to acquire it. People know if its power. People know if its importance. Its significance and what it stands for.

When you learn to build your mental state of the capability of getting wealth, you learn to build your mind. You learn to develop and enhance muscles that exercise your faith to receive wealth. A wise man seeks wisdom. Wisdom gives you the insight that you need to get wealth. When you chase wisdom, you chase knowledge. You chase the education you need to maneuver you through the channels of life. Learning to build your state of mind is key to getting wealth. Wealth is not given to most in which it is earned the old fashion way, through hard work. Many who have acquired understand the importance of the tithe. They understand the importance of giving their first 10 percent to God.

Malachi 3:10 (King James Version)
10Bring ye all the tithes into the storehouse, that there may be meat in mine house, and prove me now herewith, saith the LORD of hosts, if I will not open you the windows of heaven, and pour you out a blessing, that there shall not be room enough to receive it.

The money is which you receive does not belong to you. This money belongs to God. It is God who granted you your job. It is God who put money in your pocket. It is God who gave you the strength to achieve.

We talked about building our state of mind. You must learn the way you change the way you think. Instead of saying I cannot afford it, put into practice how can I afford it. You acquire the things that you want out of life, by the way that you think. The way that you see yourself, the way that you view yourself. Wealth is acquired both alone and in teams. Wealth comes in all different forms and fashions. Although wealth can be both a limited supply and abundance it ultimately creates freedom. Wealth comes in the form of power. Wealth helps to define the person you are. The person that you have grown to be, and the person you will soon become. You cannot only allow wealth to define the person you are. God has gives you the power to get wealth because he feels he can trust you with the currency. God feels you are trustworthy in eyes of the Lord to accomplish the goals, plans, and ideas that you have for yourself that go along with the kingdom of God. God will not give you anything that you cannot handle. God gives people that get wealth to those people that he can trust. Those people that carry out his will and keep it. A person that acquires wealth is responsible with their time. They are on time and keep track of where their time is going. These people have created a self-discipline within them that allows them to develop their mental mindset. This is why we pray and meditate on those scriptures throughout the bible the scriptures throughout the bible guide us to the plans that God has in store for us. God trust that you will do his will. He trusts that you will listen to his plans and trust the avenues in which he is guiding you towards.

The curse of poverty is sent on you to keep you away from God's best, and keep you away from your plans to get wealth. Wealth is given to people who are responsible, people who do the right thing to what's given to them.

Building your state of mind requires you building yourself. In the kingdom of heaven there is great supply of wealth. There is a limited supply of wealth on earth because earth is temporary. It doesn't last forever. Remember we were sent here temporarily for a purpose or mission in life to save lives. Your wealth says a lot about the person you are. Its says a lot about how you value your money. Wealth is more than just balancing a checkbook. Wealth sets the stage for purchasing power. When you hold the power to purchase items, you purchase items that will make you more powerful. You do not purchase items that will altar your power towards the plans that God has in store for you. You never want to altar your state of mind. Your state of mind defines the dept of volume of money your have acquired. It says a lot about the way you view your money and the plans that you have to get money. There are many people that were born to get money. People that can create revenues streams of money to create more pools of money that flow through the hands of people.

Many people feel money or wealth is an evil form of currency. God knows that you have plans to acquire wealth in your lifetime. God will not give you anything that you cannot handle. Many people that acquire wealth go through personal stress problems. The ups and downs of getting money through a political system is too much for them to handle. Your wealth is part a of a network state of mind that come together to acquire assets. It is important to know the difference between an asset and liability. With your state of mind, train yourself to acquire assets and not liabilities. Assets put money in your pocket. Liabilities take money out of your pocket. You must train your mind to acquire assets.

Besides the curse of poverty, many people fail to acquire wealth because they fail train their state of mind. They fail to train their mind to see assets instead of liabilities. You cannot focus on what the world might say about you. God says that you are a child of the highest God. You have been called out before the foundation of the world. God loves you more than you can imagine.

The reason you have been broke in your past is because you have failed to change the way that you think about money. You have failed to read books, take classes, and study ways to make money in your field. When you are worried about the things of the world you cannot focus on the plans that God has in store for you.

You have to be able to take nothing and make something. You learn to work the well without working thrust till you die. The minute you change the way you think you will begin to see the favor of God working on your behalf. Wealth can start with something as simple as an idea. Your ideas are very powerful thoughts. They help to make up the world.

Wealth says a lot about the person you are. It says a lot about the person that you have grown to be. The problem with ordinary schools is, it doesn't teach you the power to get wealth. You must acquire this information from going to classes or boot camps.

When you are at peace with yourself and have control of your state of mind you hold a better lasting chance to getting wealth.

God is looking for people who will follow him. These are the people that God will bless. These are the people that will see wealth. The people who seek it. What you do in your free time, determines your future.

Psalm 112:3 (King James Version)
3Wealth and riches shall be in his house: and his righteousness endured forever.

God says that you shall have wealth. No matter how much money you have something always takes you back to the time that you were broke. To the time that you had no money. When your pockets were filled with a lot of lent. You are always careful how you spend your money because you do not want to go broke. There are plenty of rags to riches stories of celebrities and people that have acquired great wealth throughout their lifetime. These people have trained their mind to acquire wealth. It takes a trained mind to acquire wealth. One must develop and enhance their skills towards the art of making money. One must have no distractions or occurrences of problems before becoming totally at peace with oneself. During the actual process of getting money many problems go wrong as the adversary tries to keep you away from your destiny or the plans that God has in store for you.

Proverbs 10:15 (King James Version)
15The rich man's wealth is his strong city: the destruction of the poor is their poverty.

There is wealth in the places in which you dwell. God gives you the power to get wealth because it is a part of your destiny.

Proverbs 19:4 (King James Version)
4 Wealth market many friends; but the poor is separated from his neighbor.

Wealth attracts light. It attracts friends and family from many nations. No one likes to be broke. The situational outcome or result of being broke is driving factor to ones goals to complete a level of success that has not been reached yet. There is motivation in being broke. One does not want to live this current standard of life to which one feels uncomfortable or not their best allows one to reach success through trail and error. Many different failures come through trying to reach success.

When you are wealthy you have an abundant spirit about you. Your spirit rains down from the heavens allowing you to accomplish the goals, dreams, and plans that God has in store for you. You should never run the risk of allowing someone to control your mind. The adversary tries to control your mind because he knows if he can, he can control you. When you change your mind your go through an internal transformation. You have now renewed your mind. You have transformed how to internally think. It is a transformation of your internal thoughts. You must guard your mind to what your listen to, what you say, and what you are thinking. The adversary loves to fight you in your mind. Your mind is one of the most powerful assets that you hold. We talked earlier about training our mind to acquire assets. The most powerful asset that you will hold, you already have. God has given you a mind to think. This is the reason the adversary tries to out think you towards your plans that God has in store for you. As you begin to renew your mind, you begin to meditate on those things that are the fruit of the spirit.

Wealth is a network. It's a network of currency that is waiting to be tapped into. True wealth is in the kingdom of heaven. A true Christian builds wealth in the kingdom of heaven. The kingdom of heaven is eternal in which it lasts forever. God will not give the power to gain wealth if he did not think that you could handle it. God gives wealth to people that he can trust. People that will get the job done. People that will live with honor, courage, and integrity. These people are the people that relieve their lucky break in life. Know that God gives you the power to get wealth. God is a good God.

CHAPTER 23

Forgiveness

As a Christian believer, you need to learn to forgive others. When do not forgive others you the risk the chance of allowing others to take control of your life. The people you do not forgive take hold of the life that you are living. The certain tasks, criteria, or verdict of the situation is corrupted. Its roots are embedded in you in whom its plans are to keep you from God's best. We all are seeking to live a life that goes according to the plans that God has in store for you.

Forgiveness comes from a meet heart. One that excuses the faults of others. Many people do things that need to be forgiven. Things that are your fault and things that are not your fault. Whatever the reason may be, you need to learn forgiveness. You cannot allow a person to take rule of your life. You are in control of your life and no one else. You hold the power to forgive. You hold the power to control your destiny. When you forgive you is the bigger person. You are saying to yourself that you do not sweat the small things. Rather big or small at some point in you're life you need to learn to forgive. Everything happens for a reason. It happens as part of your destiny. Well why do unfair things happen to good people. Some things are result of negative karma sent from the universe that is making its place. These negative happenings are not welcome. Another reason unfair things happen, is people have been out of the word of God for to long. We often become distant from God. We allow the happenings of the world to take control of our lives. We get involved in the current events of the world in which we are too busy for God. You should always have time for God. You are never too busy to make time for God. God is the reason for your existence. He is the reason in which you are living. It's important to make time with God.

Some of you may have to grow closer to God in order to forgive. Forgiveness is a deed that comes from the heart. It's how you view yourself along with the way that you view others. You have to forgive those people that have done you wrong throughout life. This does not mean that you have to agree with them, get along with them, or even like them. But it is important to learn how to forgive the people that have done you wrong.

Ephesians 4:32 (King James Version)
32And are ye kind one to another, tenderhearted, forgiving one another, even as God for Christ's sake hath forgiven you.

Christ has forgiven you for the sins that you have committed throughout life. We all sin. We all make mistakes. We all fall short of the glory of God and the plans that God has in store for us. As a Christian believer you have to hold your head up high and know that you are a child of the highest God. God has set you apart from the world to complete a mission in you. To complete a purpose. It read in the scripture Ephesians 4:32, forgiveness requires a tender heart. It requires you to set your feeling aside. No anger, no depression, no heartache, no pain, worries, and no fear. When you forgive you let go of burdens, strife, and strong holds that have been holding you back throughout life. Burdens, strife, and strong holds come from the adversary. It's a way the adversary can allow you to feed into his hand in the plans that he has in store for you. The adversary has plans the same as God does. Remember the adversary is trying to sell your soul. He knows that if he can keep you away from the plans that God has in store for you he can keep you away from God. Keep you away from building a relationship with God. Building a relationship with God is key to reaching your destiny.

You may have people that have hurt you in the past. People that have let you down and done you wrong throughout life. It is not up to you to hold that against them. God does not want you to get revenge, pay them back, or try to break even with them. This is left up to God. The bible says vengeance is mine said the Lord.

Romans 12:19 (New King James Version)
19 Beloved, do not avenge yourselves, but *rather* give place to wrath; for it is written, *"Vengeance is Mine, I will repay,"*[a] *says the Lord.*

You know plenty about the bible. In your forgiveness you can teach the person or people that have hurt you the truth of God word. You can show them the promises that God has in store for them these people are blind and cannot see. They have been hurt in their past which is the reason in which they feel they need to harm others. Their soul has not been saved. They have not tapped into the spiritual intelligence that God has to offer. These people are in the dark. You have the light that shines through you. The reason people are attracted to you is because they see the light that you have in you. They want the light. They want what you have. They cannot understand why they can't have the same life that you live. It is up to you to save these individuals no matter how they have treated you in the past. This is why we must forgive. This is why we must save lives. God needs you to draw them closer to the kingdom of God so that we all may be in alignment and harmony with the plans that God has in store for us. God needs for you to be the bigger person. It takes a child of God to become the bigger person throughout the world. The world has so much to offer. There are so many different options, choices, and avenues to explore.

When you don't forgive you end up holding your life up. Your life cannot progress. There is no evolutional change to the forward progression of the state of which your mind must succeed. You become a slave to your burden. Your burden, strife, and strong holds take over your life. The burden enters your body and corrupts your soul. It eats at your insides. The is the plans of the adversary. It's the way the adversary try's to kill you. We know that the adversary comes to kill, steal, and destroy. It's the way of the adversary. It has not always been the way of the adversary. The adversary was once an angel named Michael. He belonged to the kingdom of God. The adversary wanted more control and more power, but the God did not grant him that power. When God saw that the adversary was attempting to take control of the kingdom of heaven, God kicked him out. The adversary then fled to earth which he began a life. A life of murder, crime, kidnapping, violence, and thievery. The adversary saw that he could not live the life that he wanted, tried to take control of God kingdom and he was punished for it. I do not know if God has forgiven the adversary. That is such a deed thought, but I'm sure he has. Not saying that God is for the adversary, but I'm sure that God has forgiving him for his ways. God warns us of the ways of the adversary. The adversary doesn't care about you or your life. The adversary's main goal other than killing you is to allow you to become a slave for him in his kingdom.

When you allow burdens to weigh you down, you miss the promises that God has in store for you. You are to busy worrying about what others have done for you, you cannot see the plans that God has in store for you that allow you to reach your destiny. These are the exact plans of the adversary. He will try to do anything to keep you away from the plans that God has in store for you. He knows that God has great things in store for you, which is why he works hard at not allowing you to forgive those who have done you wrong throughout life.

Forgiveness comes from the heart. It comes from being obedient to God. From listening and caring out the plans that God have told you. You cannot carry out the plans that God has in store for you when you do not listen. God wants you to be obedient to him. He wants you to listen to his plans. Do not worry what others may say of you. Other people don't define you. You define yourself. You control your destiny. Greater is he that is in you, than he that is in the world.

1 John 4:4 (King James Version)
4Ye are of God, little children, and have overcome them: because greater is he that is in you, than he that is in the world.

God has already overcome the world. You are free from sin. You now live in victory. You do not have to go around living in defeat the rest of your life.

We know that Jesus died for your sins. Jesus Christ forgave you for every sin that you committed when he died on the cross. This was Jesus' way of saying I love you. Jesus wanted to forgive you for the sins that you commit throughout your lifetime. We all know that we commit sins throughout our life. It's a part of life. This does not make it right. God is not saying to go out and sin on purpose. God wants you to live a life of victory, integrity, and honor. It's the way of the Lord. Its part of the plan that God has in store for you. We continually talk about the plans that God has in store four you because it is important to live your life by them. Your life will not be complete any other way. People wonder why they cannot get their life together, its because they are attempting to live a life without God. God's love for you stretches out further than you can imagine. His love is like a deep ocean. God has cast out your sins further than the east is from the west. This is why you live above the curse. You are free from the curse. The adversary has no control over your life if you do not allow him. I did not say that he doesn't have control over your life because he will if you allow him. If you keep feeding into his hands through sin, you will soon become a slave for the adversary. Do not allow the adversary the chance to win your soul over. Do the things that you know are right in your heart.

Forgiveness requires a meek heart. It requires you to become the bigger person. We continually talk about being the bigger person because God wants you to be. God wants you to lead be example. Some people are leaders in life and some people are followers. Whatever your aspect may be, do it to the best of your ability. If you are a leader be the best leader that you can be. If you are a follower be the best follower you can be. Some people think leaders are the best. I will let you in on a little secret. In order to be a leader you must be a follower. You must follow in the footsteps of the people that laid the blueprint out for you. God needs for you to play your role in society. You cannot be afraid of what others may say of you, what others may think of you, and how others will respond. You simply play your role. You do you. Doing you allows you to take control of your life. It allows you to take control of the strong holds the adversary try's to put on you. Sure people will do you wrong. Sure people will talk behind your back. Will tell you lie, but you know that you are a child of the highest God. You know that you have been set apart from the world in which you live above the curse of poverty. You may not have everything that you want, but you have your health and your strength. You have the basic necessities of life. You cannot achieve more, get more, or accomplish more until you start being thankful for the things that you have in life now. In what ways have you thanked God for the blessings that you have now. You cannot say that God has not blessed you in your life. There are hundred of ways that God has blessed you. Make a list of all the ways God has blessed you. In what ways has God been good to you and what ways are you thankful for them. How are you thankful for the people that God has put in your life? What obstacles have you overcome? In what ways has God helped you to forgive someone?

Forgives

S takes character. It allows you to show your true colors. That you are indeed the bigger person in life. God loves when his children forgive. Maybe someone has forgiven you. Maybe they haven't. I pray they will read this and learn the importance of forgiving. Learn the importance of allowing their life to flow, so that burdens will not hold them up. God wants you to succeed. God wants you to live your life in victory. You do not have to go around in defeat. You now live above the curse. Learn to forgive the people around you. Learn to take the challenge in life. God has a plan for your life and it all starts with you. God wants you to live your life in victory. God wants you to do the right things. Help someone along the way. Lead by example. Set the example. You are child of the highest God and God loves you. God is good God.

CHAPTER 24

Releasing Your Burdens

There is a certain freedom you feel when you release the burdens that take hold of you. As a Christian believer the burdens that you hold help to define the destiny in which you will receive. The adversary attempts to place burdens in your life to keep you away from the plans that God has in store for you. We all have fallen short of the glory of God throughout our life. When you attempt to live a life without God, you risk taking on burdens that keep you away from God's best. God wants the best for you and so should you.

2 Kings 9:25 (King James Version)
25Then said Jehu to Biker his captain, Take up, and cast him in the portion of the field of Jabot the Jezreelite: for remember how that, when I and thou rode together after Ahab his father, the LORD laid this burden upon him;

In this scripture God places a heavy burden on him. This is what happens when you attempt to live a life without Christ. You can feel heaviness in your heart, mind, body, soul, and spirit. You know that something is not right. Your life does not flow in alignment and harmony with the plans that God has in store for you. Your life flows when you are living a life a for God.

To often we try to compare our lives to others. We receive burden from the Lord or the adversary, we know our life is not right and we try to compare it to others. You say to yourself in what ways is my life better than his? Why does he have more? Why do I go through all of these problems? Its part of human nature that you compare yourself to others. As a Christian believer, God does not want you to compare your life to anyone else's. God needs for you to live your life becoming a better you. God needs for you to live your life according to the principals in God's word. When you are disobedient to God, God takes his hand of favor off of you. This opens the door for burden, strife, and strong holds to come into your life. The adversary is alive in full affect seeking to devour that he can.

1 Peter 5:8 (New King James Version)
8 Be sober, be vigilant; because [a] your adversary the devil walks about like a roaring lion, seeking whom he may devour.

When you live a life with burden, strife, and strong holds it is harder to live a life for God. You draw closer to God when you have burden in your life. Your body's natural response is to get rid of the burden in which your body has now taken on. Your body was designed to live in prosperity not failure. Failure is a burden or curse that is put on you by the adversary. The adversary does not want you to make it. We know that he attempts to keep us away from God's best.

When you are living a life that goes according to God's best you do not have to worry about receiving heartache, pain, and misery. God knows that he loves you; this is why God has called his only son to save you from the world.

The burden and strife that you feel I sent from the adversary, because he knows that God has something greater in store for you. He knows that you are part of a plan. You belong to the kingdom of God. God has called you out before the foundation of the world.

Ephesians 1:4 (New King James Version)
**4 just as He chose us in Him before the foundation of the
world, that we should be holy and without blame before Him
in love,**

This is mentioned several times in this book to illustrate
the plans that God has in store for you. When you live a life of
burden you find yourself going in circles not receiving the fruit
of the spirit that God has in store for you. You cannot hear from
God, because you are to busy trying to release the burden that
you have upon yourself.

You release the burden in your life by going to God in prayer.
We pray to God to establish a covenant relationship that is part
of an incorruptible seed that cannot be broken. God's love for
you stretches out further than you can imagine. God does not
want to see you go in circles. God wants to see you living your
best life now. We recommend Joel Osteen "Your Best Life Now",
to living a life that has God's best for you. In "Your Best Life
Now," you learn seven steps that place you on the road to victory.
Enlarge Your Vision, Develop a Healthy Self-Image, Discover the
Power of Your Thoughts and Words, Let go of the Past, Find
Strength Through Adversity, and Live to Give, and Choose to
Be Happy. These are all steps that will place you on your road to
victory. We know that the adversary does not want us to make
it. This is the reason he works so hard to keep you away from
the plan that God has in store for you. He knows that God has
great things in store for you. He knows that you are God's best.
You have something to offer the world. When you live in strife,
the adversary try's to take away the seed that you hold to offer to
the world. Numerous preachers such as Joel and Victoria Osteen,
Jessie Duplantis, Tim Story, Walter Hallam, Kenneth and Gloria
Copeland, Creflo Dollar, T D Jakes, Rick Warren, Paula White,
Benny Hinn, Bill Winston, Rod Parsley and more preach the
importance of overcoming the adversary when he strikes. These
pastors know the importance of the power you hold through the
seeds that God has planted eternally inside of you. Remember the

seed is incorruptible, so it cannot be broken. God has made you one with him and he with you.

Millions of people throughout the world live there live in depression, misery, heartache, and pain because they do not know how to release the burden that the adversary has placed in their life. Living your to the best of your ability in the eyes of God is not always easy. It takes a lot out of you. It takes a lot for you to live your life to be the best. You should never be worried about how someone else is living his or her life. You should never get in the trap of comparing your life to others. God has granted you life so that you may live it more abundantly. God did not plan for you to live in defeat. God has great plans for your life; it says it here in the scripture.

Jeremiah 29:11 (King James Version)
11For I know the thoughts that I think toward you, saith the LORD, thoughts of peace, and not of evil, to give you an expected end.

Long before you were born God planned for you to prosper. God did not plan for you to live in defeat. TO often we listen to the lies of the adversary and the people around us, putting our faith in man instead of God. You are a child of the highest God. When we receive burden and strife we simply go to God in prayer. God does not need for you to try to handle all of your problems on your own. God needs for you to come to him in prayer. Some of you have been so distant from God that you are afraid to go back. You are afraid to know what he might think. Some of you feel that you have missed up so bad, you are afraid to know how God will react. God still loves you. We all fall short of the glory of God. No sin is greater than the other. We all sin and we all fall short of the glory of God. God loves you today, tomorrow, and forever. His love runs deep for you. When you have fallen short of the glory of God, receive burden, and strife, go to God in prayer. Release your burdens to the Lord. Tell God your problems. This allows you to communicate with God one on one with the issues that you are now facing. I know many of you are facing depression, sicknesses, death, misery, heartache, pain, and many more serious life issues that need to be resolved. Let me tell you, you cannot take on these problems by yourself. You need the help and the power of all might God. God has the ability to move mountains.

Mark 11:23 (King James Version)
23For verily I say unto you, That whosoever shall say unto this mountain, Be thou removed, and be thou cast into the sea; and shall not doubt in his heart, but shall believe that those things which he saith shall come to pass; he shall have whatsoever he saith.

This is the power that you hold when you believe in God. There is nothing the adversary can do to keep you away from the plans that God has in store for you.

When you pray to God you lift up a heavy burden that has been holding you back. Simply go to God in prayer. Remember we always pray through Jesus, so we start our prayer "in the name of your son Jesus Christ or end them with "in the name of your son Jesus. Simply say, In the name of your son Jesus Christ, God all mighty I lift this prayer up to you. I pray for this heavy burden that is keeping me from being God best. I pray that you will come into my heart and show me the way. I know that I have not been living my life according to the plans of your word, but I repent of my sins. When you repent of your sins, you are washing away all of your sins. God help me to become a better person. Help me to draw closer to you. Help me to know the plans that you have in store for me. I surrender my life to Christ knowing that Jesus has died on the cross for our sins. I thank you for sacrifice of his life for all of mankind. I pray that I will no longer heave heartache, pain, misery, death, depression, and suffering throughout the world. Help me to achieve the goals and dreams that I want to achieve. Help me to do your works in which I am a servant of the Lord. God all mighty, I lift this prayer up to you in the name of your son Jesus Christ. Amen. That's all you have to do! It's that simple. God loves when you come to him in prayer. In that prayer we surrendered our life to Christ. We said that we are living our life for God and no one else. We also allowed God the opportunity to come into our life and release the burdens that the adversary has placed in our life. You can feel a sense of relieve over your heart when you are doing the works of God. You can feel a sense of relieve when you are doing the works of the Lord. God loves you more than you can imagine. This is why we must go to God in prayer. This is why we must lift up our problems to the Lord. We cannot face this battle alone. We need the help of all mighty God. God was with Noah when he built the ark. God was with Moses when he parted the red sea. God was with David when he defeated Goliath. You do not face the world alone, only if you allow yourself. God is with you every step of the way.

When you do not live your life for God, God will take his hand of favor off of you. This occurs when we are disobedient to God. This brings burden, strife, and strongholds. These strong holds weigh us down. They prevent us from receiving God's best. God will not give you more than you can handle throughout life. God knows what you are capable of.

When you learn to trust God, you learn to trust yourself. You learn to trust the plans that God has in store for you. You learn to trust what God will do for you. You begin to conform yourself into the ways of the kingdom of God instead of the world. You cannot spend your days worrying about other people around you. You have your own life to get together. This does not mean ignore them or do not lend out a hand to help them, but you cannot handle everyone else problems. God has their problems under control. The more time you spend with God, spend in prayer, and spend reading the bible the more results you will see working in your favor. You should avoid being a hypocrite. Avoid saying one thing and doing another. This is a person who is unstable in their ways. They say they are a Christian, but live their life to the world's standards. God has so much to show you. So much to reveal to you. It's all-apart of the plan that God has in store for you. God wants you to be prosperous. He wants you to live in abundance. You do not have to go around in defeat. God has defeat the curse. You now live in victory. You are a child of the highest God. You have been set out apart from the world and called out before the foundation of the world for a purpose. A mission. A mission to save every life and soul that exists. This is the plan that God has in store for you so that you may have eternal life. God is a good God.

CHAPTER 25

Power

All throughout this book we have been talking about the power that you hold. Your power comes from God. God instructs his Christian believer to be strong in the Lord and the power of his might.

Ephesians 6:10 (New King James Version)
10 Finally, my brethren, be strong in the Lord and in the power of His might.

This is the power that God has equipped you with. This is the power that God has in store for you. All you see the power of God at work. You see it on the job, in the church, at home, when you're out, and in many different places. God has equipped us with power to carry out the mission of God. Your power comes from within. It comes from with your heart, mind, body, soul, and spirit. It's the power that God has equipped you with. The powers you have been given to you are birth. It's in your genes; it's in the way you talk, the way you move, and the way that you live your life for God. You power enables you to do great things on the face of the earth. God has the power to move mountains. God can do many amazing things at the touch of his hand. This is all done in the power of your faith through Christ.

Your faith is enabled by power. The power you have to believe that you can achieve. Power doesn't come and go. It is displayed through the universe as a universal force that exists when slecked. You hold the power to control your power. The power that you have within you defines your strength. It defines the strength that you have for yourself. No one man should have all that power. Power is given to you through trust through God.

Man can do great things with power, which is the reason that God has trusted us with it. God gave manpower for a reason. To have dominion over creations. Creations that exist in which should be controlled by the power given to man. You control the power of situations for the direct involvement of your conscious.

God gave you power because he knew that he could trust you in every situation of your life. You should never let anyone have control over your power. A person that attempts to control your power feel less empowered himself or herself in the sense that there life does not feel complete. Their strength is lost and their soul is seeking to find itself. The adversary has drained all the power from your system in which you hold for yourself. The world often takes a lot out of us. As we share our testimonies of living matters to those we truly care, life takes a lot out of us. Your soul bleeds life to the universe as it operates. You are working for God. You are a servant to the Lord and to God. We are sent here to carry out the mission in which God instruct us with. This is all done through the power of God. The power that God has enabled us to complete the mission through Christ. God has given you power for a reason. To complete a mission through Christ.

We begin to tame the power that we have in us. You must hone your skills towards the power that was given to you. You must learn how to control it. How to use it is as leverage. How to use it to receive the things that you want most out of life from your inner desires to satisfy your soul. Your soul craves for the things that you want most out of life. Your conscious reads your soul and finds that your soul seeking the things that you want most out of life. Your body then reacts to your soul and conscious and seeks ways to satisfy the need. This is part of the progressive state of mind of pleasing your wants and needs. It's common that we seek after the things that we want most out of life. This is a part of life. It's a part of the way we were designed that defines our human conscious. This is all a part of the power through conscious motion of waves that exist throughout the universe. When you feed your soul you feed your conscious. You feed a living spiritual organism that exists through your waves in your mind. You hold the power to feed your soul. You hold the power to control your power.

Once your begin to tame or control your power, you begin to self discipline yourself for greatness. You have taken the time to master your power. You have taken the time to discipline yourself for the production that will take place. There is power in heaven and hell. The reality effect of the results of consequences of ones action that takes place in heaven is done through power. This is why the adversary attempts to control all the power. Remember the adversary ounces lived in heaven. The adversary wanted more power and more control which is the reason in which God casted him down to earth. God knew that it was too much power for one living creature to hold. God knew his greed, pride, and arrogance the adversary held within, which is the reasons why he was cast down to earth.

God allows you to control your power in order to control yourself. When you learn to control your power, you learn to control yourself. You control your destiny, plans, actions, and conscious. The power you hold holds great results. Power helps you to be seen more in the light. When you have no power you are in the dark. Your mental state becomes weak. You draw away from the strength you once had. The adversary drains you from your power. The universe also drains you from this same power. This is the reason we need rest at night. You must restore the power that you hold for yourself. Power comes in the sense of fatigueless. You can easily tire yourself out or drain your power. You must restore your power through sleep. When you awake your power will come again.

We talk about power because it enables us to gain greatness in life. Most dynamic scenarios in life are done through power. The power to control oneself and the power to control situations that occur. God gave you power because he wanted you to have dominion over your life. Dominion of your family at what matters to you the most. You control your power through controlling yourself.

Power is God made. It is also human made. This is the reason why God gave manpower. When you have power you can control. You control the events, situations, and obstacles that occur throughout your life. You can control situations and their outcomes. You can plan for success or ways to avoid failure. You hold the power to make things work. Outcomes that will happen in your favor. God will not give you more than you can handle. You should never make the mistake of abusing your power. This is the reason satin power was stripped from him. He was stripped of his title of an angel. God has the ultimate power. His kingdom is powerful. His love is strong. No one man can have all the power.

Your acquire power to become stronger. God planned for you to use your power to the best of your ability. Use it to help the people in your environment. You hold the power to get wealth, money, riches, family, happiness, prosperity, and abundance. God's word is the most power book of literature ever published. It holds all the answers to life. It is blueprint for your life in which you should live your life accordingly. God wrote the bible so that we may read it, know it, and live it. It's all a part of the plans that God has in store for you. God gives us power to accomplish the tasks that we have at hand. God never needs for you to abuse your power.

We often abuse our power by gain too much. The materialistic things that our soul desires are given to us through obedience. You often risk the chance of wanting more. Your inner self seeks for more abusing the power to get wealth, happiness, family, and abundance. We abuse our power through our inner desires. This is why it is so important to be thankful for the things that God has blessed us with. You gain true power through meditation.

Meditation to God or prayer. God holds the answers to the power of your prayers. Your prayer is more powerful than you think. This is your way to outsmart the adversary. You now become part of an agreement to God to accomplish the prayers that you have for yourself. God moves mountains through the power of prayers. Your prayers mean the most to God. This is God's way of building a personal relationship with him. We often talk about the importance of building a relationship with God. This the way that you get to know God. A way to get to know the person that created you. God wants to know your wants and your needs. We say wants and needs because every want is not a need. God grants you both wants and needs, as you are obedient to him in which you carry out the plans that God has in store for you. You hold the key to very powerful results.

Meditate on your most inner thoughts. Thoughts that move you the most. Then come to a reality. See yourself make your actions known to God. This means go to God in prayer. Lift up the people around you, the people that God has placed in your life for reason. Some people for you to help, some people to receive help from. God puts people in your life so that you may help them. This is the power that you. People see the power in you. People see the light that you hold within you, which is the reason they are attracted to you. The light that you hold is powerful. It moves the kingdom of God. As you pray to God you receive power through your prayers. There is deliverance in your prayers. God delivers you out of storms that are not God's best for your heart, mind, body, soul, and spirit. Your soul becomes more powerful as you're pray. As you lift up whets on your heart, God grants you the power to accomplish the tasks that you have set at hand.

We often wonder how we will receive the power to make it through the day. God gives you the power to get through your days. This is why we thank God for it. We thank God when we have had a good day. We thank God when he is good to us. We thank God for the blessings that we have in our life. God blesses those people that draw closet to him and his word. God blesses people that continue to seek him. God's word says that we will find him when we seek him with our whole heart.

Jeremiah 29:13 (King James Version)
13And ye shall seek me, and find me, when ye shall search for me with all your heart.

You find power when you find God. You find a key to life that unlocks all the strong holds that have been holding you back. A heavy burden is released off of you when you discover the power God has in store for you. God then takes control of your life. Your whole life your soul has been searching for God. You have been too busy allowing the adversary to strip you of your power. Your soul becomes lost in which it is stranger to God. You only know the things of this world. Your job is to store up treasures in heaven.

Matthew 6:20 (King James Version)
20But lay up for you treasures in heaven, where neither moth nor rust doth corrupt, and where thieves do not break through nor steal:

This is why God wants you to store treasures in heaven. God is knows you every need. This is why we draw closer to him. God begins to reveal his plans to us, as we draw closer to him and begin to know him. God knows your every wildest dream. He knows every home you want to live in, every car you want to drive, every homerun you want to hit, and every touchdown you want to score. He knows your needs. God knew that plans that he had in store for you long before you existed. This is why God's plans never fail. It's all a part of the power of God.

When you learn to tap into your power, you begin to see the universe moving your favor. God begins to align breaks up in your favor. This is the power that God holds for you. Never abuse you power. Do not risk the chance of having your power striped from you. This can and will happen if you allow it. Power is given to people who are obedient to God. People with integrity, morals, and values. This is the reason the president holds so much power. God knows the power needed to move nation. We must get our country back on the right track in a sense that we are respected again. People have lost respect in our country and for our country. Respect will return as the power returns. The power you hold allows you to move nations. God is a good God.

CHAPTER 26

Breakthrough

As a Christian believer, God has your breakthrough for you. Your breakthrough with is right around the corner. All throughout life individuals are waiting for their breakthrough. Breakthrough's come in there due season. Breakthrough's come when God needs them to come. And breakthrough's come with an overflow of abundance.

Breakthrough's come for those who are ready for them, those who are prepared for the anointing of the blessing. God is ready to release his anointing where you will not have room enough to receive within his kingdom. (Malachi 3:10) (pour out blessings where you will not have room enough to receive) Breakthrough's are for all people. Breakthroughs happen everyday to ordinary people who are ready to receive them.

You have to be ready to receive them. You have to be ready in the spirit, equipped in the spirit, and anointed in the spirit of God. Maybe you are ready for a breakthrough on the job, in school, in life, or with, your breakthrough is right around the corner. Your breakthrough is right in front of you, you just have to reach out and grab. God is ready to release his anointing for those who are ready and meek enough to receive. There is nothing the adversary can do. There is nothing the devil can do to steal your breakthrough, your victory. It's all-apart of the plans for the

Sean Maddox

kingdom of God. You must continue to stay in prayer, stay in the anointed and stay in the spirit of God to receive the fullness in the spirit for all mighty God. Your breakthrough comes through preparation, timing, and readiness. One has to train one's mind to be prepared for what awaits one.

There is a wealth of opportunity for millions of Christian believers that are equipped in the spirit. This is the wealth of the spirit that you have within you in which you will overflow with abundance when your breakthrough comes. You must not faint.

Galatians 6:9 And let us not be weary in well doing: for in due season we shall reap, if we faint not. God is saying to not be tired from your outward appearance of work that you apply to life, which is good works. God see's your God works, he see's all of the good things that you put out into the kingdom of God from your heart in which you have great intentions for.

God is saying in your due season you shall have your reward. We talk about rewards because God wants you to be rewarded for your labors while on earth. God wants you to have a good time before we go to heaven and have a great time.

Matthew 5:12 Rejoice and be exceeding glad: for great is your reward in heaven: for so persecuted that the prophets which were before you. God says to rejoice and be glad. God wants you to be happy! He wants you to release the anger, burden and strife that you feel. The burden, strife, and anger you feel is like a poison that eats up your eternal body. A poison that is brought on by the best of you that spreads and somehow in a way gets the best of you. God says great is your reward in heaven.

God has plans to reward you great in heaven. This is a promise from God. Its another promise from God from the many promises that God has made throughout the bible. The bible is filled with promises. Promises to give you a hope, future God see's your intentions, he see's your actions. God see's the heart, intentions, and actions of your children, yourself, and the people around you. In order to receive your breakthrough you must continue practice at the craft in which you have. You must continue to do those things that are right. Learn to get back into your mode. Get into your mode of doing the right thing. It's easy to get out of your mode of doing the wrong things. It natural and it happens from time to time. We all get off track. Its important to stay on track for the plans that God has in store for us.

I say it time and time again Jeremiah 29:11 For I know the thoughts that I think of you saith the Lord, thoughts of peace and not of evil, to give you an expected end. God wants to give you an expected end a promising future, that is everlasting but you must believe this with all of your heart. You must not faint. You must continue to do the right things. Those things that are honoring to God. Good things come along to those who are prepared. Preparation is the key to success in this face-paced world that we live in today. One's that are prepared are destined to succeed and one's who are not prepared are destined to fail. There is a valuable lesson learned for those who fail. Failure can be part of your breakthrough.

Millions of individuals fail before they receive their breakthrough. In fact before any form of success failure often occurs so your breakthrough is right around the corner after a sure failure. In no way form of fashion are we promoting failure or saying that failure is okay or an option. We are simply saying to not be afraid of failure. Do not be afraid of failing. Get out of your comfort zone and get in your zone. To often we get into a mode of comfort in which we become to relaxed allowing our heart, mind, body, and soul to enter into a mode of laziness that pulls us away from the recent activity that has our attention that is part of our success in breakthrough. Your breakthrough is big and your breakthrough is important to God Love what I do. I receive a comfort from pouring out my heart to God receive the fruit of the spirit in whole. The bible has so many promises, scriptures, quotes, and analogies to life that are meant for praise, rejoice, and our hearts to help us along our path, journey, and daily life's. You have to break out of the mentality of if God wanted you to have it you would have it. Because God does want you to have it. God wants you to be prosperous! God wants you to live in victory.

Isaiah 25:8 He swallow up death in victory and the Lord God will wipe away tears from off all faces and the rebuke of his people shall he take away from off all the earth for the Lord hath spoken it. God says that he swallows up death in victory. This is the victory that we celebrate to overcome the kingdom of God. This is the celebration of victory that we have overcome death! Death is not one meant to destroy, but to celebrate one's life for all one has achieved. God promises to wipe away all tears from all faces. You no longer have to cry. You no longer have to worry. You can now live in victory. These are the plans for God. Victory of the celebration of life. Celebration of the anointing, celebration of your breakthrough. God promises to rebuke those that come against you.

You do not have to worry about those people that come against you or persecute you. You can feel it in the air, the spirit of God anointing your breakthrough. Everywhere you go you can feel the presence of God. God is everywhere. God has a anointing about him that will cause you to prosper and be in health.

3 John 1:2 Beloved, I wish above all things that thou mayest prosper and be in health, even as thy soul prospereth. God is saying that you as a person wish, pray, and believe above all things. You wish above those things that are beneath you. You wish above those things that are not godly and those things that are ungodly. That thou mayest prosper and be in health even as thy soul prospereth. You will prosper and be in health. You will have good health. You will have a restore life. Your life will be filled with glory of earth and in heaven. You have an anointed life. You have a life worth living. You have a life that God has destined for success.

The spirit of God flows through you as you know that God has great things in store for you when you believe. God has equipped you with everything that you need. God has given you all that you need plus more. God has plenty. their are cups running over. Psalms 23:5 Thou prepares a table before me in the presence of mine enemies; thou anoints my head with oil; my cup rennet over.

God prepares a table, a heavenly banquets for you. When your enemies are present God protects you. The anointed of your head with oil is the anointed blessing you will receive. There is an overflow of abundance. The adversary cannot steal your pride, joy, and wealth when you stay in the word of God. God is saying to try a little harder. Try a little harder to receive your breakthrough. Your preparation comes with a prepared mind. A transformation of ones eternal thoughts. Get your mind ready, get your mind prepared for what awaits you. God has plans for you to succeed, but you must be ready. It is not going to fall in your lap, it's going to take hard work, it's going to take determination, its going to take blocking out the adversary when he try's to attack.

The adversary does not want you to make it. God needs for you to succeed and you will. God has everything layed out for you. God has everything that you need plus more. God will place people along your path that will be responsible for your breakthrough. You simply have to do the will of God. You simply have to do those things that are necessary that will help you thrust you to a new level I'm every area of your life. You have to make it happen. You are responsible for your actions. God allows you to be mature enough to make the necessary decisions that will affect your life.

Psalms 128:2 For thou shalt eat labour of thine hands: happy shalt thou be, and it shall be well with thee. You will enjoy the fruits of your labors. God wants you to enjoy your life.

Isaiah 1:19 If ye be willing and obedient, ye shall eat the good of the land. God promises that he will bless you for being obedient in which you will enjoy the fruits of your labor eating the good of the land. You will eat the good of the land and you continue to do the good works. The righteous works.

Those works, which are, right in the eyes of God and not right in the eyes of the world. God continues to give you inspiration and motivation for your aspirations. The word of God is real.

The word of God never goes void. The word of God remains constant. The word of God is the variable.

The spirit of God allows you to feel good about yourself. God continues to rain down his anointing of prosperity among you. Your breakthrough is right around the corner. You must work hard for the things that you want out of life. Nothing comes handed to you. Hard work along with preparation is needed. Your breakthrough is there, your breakthrough is awaiting you. Its part of a righteousness. Its part of a righteous spirit. God will align people in your path for your that will be responsible for helping you achieves the desired goals. You must learn to live a well-balanced lifestyle.

Balancing a work life with home life is essential for your success. Often times joggling both work and home life can leave you busy. You must learn to balance work and home life. It's healthier for you to balance your work and home life.

You must learn to relax and not let things get the best of you. You must continue to do those things that are right in the eyes of God. Those things that honor God. You must receive the fruit of the spirit. God delivers the fruit of the spirit. God places those things that you need in your path. As a Christian believer you must watch out for those individuals that will try to ruin your breakthrough. Those who try to get in the way or disturb you. God continues to bring people along your path that will help you. Those that will thrust you to a new level for your success. Your breakthrough is one of the biggest deals of your career. God has a way of putting things in black and white so that you may receive them. God continues to push you along towards the mark. Towards you're desired goals in which you need to achieve. There are times in life that we come short of the glory of God. We fall short of our shortcoming. We are all guilty of this. We all fail from time to time. God is always right on time. God is never late. God's timing is always right to which you live. You do not have to rush God. God knows what he is doing throughout the kingdom and God does what he does well. Everything will fall into place in its due season. God has everything lined up for you.

God is looking down from above waiting for you to complete your tasks. God see's all things. God see's when people are doing you wrong. You do not have to try to retaliate or get back at those who have done you wrong.

Matthew 5:44 says: Buy I say unto you, Love your enemies, bless them that curse you, do good to them that hate you, and pray for them which despitefully use you, and persecute you. God is saying that you should love your enemies. You should love those that come against you. If you live long enough you will come to a point in life that you will have enemies from time to time. You have people that come against you. People who turn against you and people that are traders. In no way form or fashion are you to fellowship with these individuals. Fellowshipping with darkness is not the plans of God. 2 Corinthians 6:14: Be ye not unequally yoked together with unbelievers: for what fellowship hath righteousness with unrighteousness? And what communion hath light with darkness? God is saying to not be yoked together with darkness. To not be yoked together with unrighteousness.

God does not want us to fellowship with unbeliever, people that are not part of the body of Christ. Light and darkness do not mix. God is light and in him is no darkness. God is saying bless them that curse you. Not in the sense that an individual will literally try to put a curse on you, but in the sense that those that literally curse you with wicked tongues. We all have had individuals that come against us. We all have had our share of adversary and adversary spirits. God says to bless them and to pray for them. Proverbs 15:1 a soft answer turned away wrath, but grievous words stir up anger. God needs for you to be gentle to those that come against you.

A soft answer turned away those things that lead to trouble. It is not the time to be cocky or try to show out of what one can do to try to taunt or impress another individual in which this leads to destruction in which destroys the kingdom of God. God is saying do good to those that come against you. The spirit of God is free and it flows through you freely. The spirit of God is also literally free. It doesn't cost anything to freely worship God.

Sean Maddox

It doesn't cost you a penny. You can receive the anointing from God through acceptant Jesus dying on the cross for you for free. It great to know that it doesn't cost anything except to accept Christ and to know that Jesus died for you. God says to pray for those that persecute you. Praying for people helps in ways that you could not imagine. Praying for people allows God to work behind the scenes. God is working behind closed doors to move the favor of God in your direction. We know that God see's everything and there is nothing to that God does not see.

Luke 6:27 says, But I say unto you which hear, Love your enemies, do good to them which hate you. 28, Bless them that curse you and pray for them, which despitefully use you. Prayer to God is all that is needed. Prayer to God is what seals the message. It seals the anointing. There are times throughout the world people will hate you. People will come against you and curse you. It happened to Jesus and friend it will happen to you. They hated Jesus for what he did. They hated Jesus for worshipping God, healing people, and do good deeds. They hated Jesus for this. For this simple fact Jesus paid the price for you. So that you may live above the curse of God. So that you may live above those things that are not of God throughout the world.

Everything flows into place. All things fit into place like a hand in a glove or your foot into a brand new pair of shoes throughout the kingdom. God see's everything. God is the headman in charge. No one comes to God but through Jesus. * you must have you must have your things in order. You must be certain of oneself or certain of yourself in every area of your life. This helps with your mental preparation. You cannot pay attention to those things of the world.

The things of the world are in a physical realm. You are now connected to the spiritual realm. God see's your heart and he see's your intentions. God will place people in your path that will help to thrust you to new levels. Everything in life happens for a reason. The adversary try's to tell you that you are not going anywhere. The adversary try's to tell you that you will not make it. God has people lined up awaiting for your breakthrough.

People that will be there to celebrate with you. People that will be there for your victories. People that will be there when you fall, when you tumble, through the ups and the downs, the peaks and valleys, the highs and the lows, and through the mountain tops. People that will be there to advice you and tell you the right things to do. God places these people in your life because it's important and its part of your breakthrough. Its part of good bringing you to a new level in your life. God is forever bringing you to new levels in your life. We are all filled with dreams, goals, and aspirations that are part of the plan for all mighty God. Your preparation along with the people God brings in your life is part of your success. You have a reward in heaven.

Matthew 5:12 says Rejoice and be exceeding glad for great is your reward in heaven: for so persecuted they the prophets, which were before you. Here is another promise throughout the bible that says great is your reward in heaven. God promises that you will have a great reward in heaven. He also goes on to say that they persecuted those that came before you so they will also persecute you. Persecute is defined as to pursue with harassing or oppressive treatment because of religion, race or beliefs. This happens because these individuals have not been saved.

They have not confessed Romans 10:9 the scripture that saves lives. That if thou shalt confess with thy mouth the Lord Jesus, and believe in thine heart that God has raised him from the dead thou shalt be saved. God continues to reveal more and more to you as you are obedient. God takes unordinary people and does ordinary things with them. Simply look all around you there are billions of talented individuals that are about to reach new levels in the their life from their talents! God has a way of showing up and showing out. God has people ready to help you. Those that are ready to join you. You have power. You have the power to make unbelievers believers. Unbelievers foreclose because they do not have the word of God that you hold. They do not have the anointing spirit, power, and abundance that you hold. You are part of their success.

You will help them to go to a new level with their walk with God. With the economy the way it is people have been forced to sacrifice. Sacrifice in their money*n sacrifice with their family, with their personal belongings, and sacrifice most importantly with their life. People are drawing more and more closer to God. There has never been a better opportunity to draw closer. God brings us closer to together during our breakthrough so that we may come closer together in all that we do as a team. God comes in the form of a team sport.

I have said it before and I will sat it again There is no "I" in team. Your breakthrough is a perfect return on investment with God, the kingdom of God, and heaven. Your partnership with God is second to none and is part of your personal relationship that you have built with God. God see's your heart and he see's your intentions in what you are doing. God is willing to restore to you anything and everything that has been los. God allows you to go to new levels because he has greater things in store for you. God does not want you to get comfortable.

Jeremiah 29:11 For I know the thoughts that I think of you saith the Lord, thoughts of peace and not evil to give you an expected end. God is saying that you go for yours. You have to power to achieve. God has given you everything that you need. God is not going to run out of resources. God has an overflow of abundance. Did not get discouraged if you see your friends, family, relatives, and co workers moving up and your not. Your time is coming if you do not faint.

Galatians 6:9 And let us not be weary in well doing: for in due season we shall reap, if we faint not. Here is another promise from God. We continue to talk about the many promises that God has. God is saying let us not be tired for the efforts of our works for our well doing. For in due season we shall reap if we not faint. That means if we do not give up! You cannot give up. You cannot afford to fall short of the glory of God even though it does happen from time to time. When this happens you must pick yourself up and dust yourself off and keep going. God has already lined up your big breaks. God teaches you to be calm allowing the spirit of God to come to you in a smooth natural sense. The spirit of God should not be rushed throughout the kingdom. It should flow natural in a real sense that you feel relaxed, rejuvenated, and anointed. The spirit of God has a rich, wealthy presence to it because it is wealthy in the spirit. It is full of purification in the sense that is healing. Its part of the healing process that the spirit of God flows upon you.

The spirit of God loves to heal. It loves to teach others, and bless others. The spirit of God is not deceiving or seducing in the sense that it opens up a gateway to those things of the adversary. The spirit of God is calm, its romantic, is soothing, and its what you need. It's a healing process in the motion. Its healing in progress and its healing in works. That spirit of God sales because it is the truth in its purest form. The purification of the word of God, the spirit of God, and the kingdom of God cleanses and purifies the world. The spirit of God is real, it authentic, genuine and holds a quality of life that is like no other. The spirit of God units to second level putting it in a long of its own. The spirit of God has a way with words that is gratifying. The spirit of God is the anointing, it is the one, its heroic, and its history. It's all apart of the breakthrough.

It's all-apart of you, because you are one with the spirit of God. It heals scars, it heals wounds, breakups and it heals hearts. The spirit of God is part of a friendly completion. A friendly competitiveness. Its part of your life in which you bring the best out of yourself. You have to be prepared for things that occur. Things do come up that can put your career on hold, cause you to alter your plans or change the direction of your plans in a different direction. The spirit of God can come amongst you like an anointed spirit like no other. You begin to go to a new level.

The spirit of God never strikes without warning. The spirit of God is a cool, calm, and gentleness. The adversary try's to break up your breakthrough. The adversary try's to get in the middle or get in between the plans that God has in store for you. The adversary try's to come in between friendships, relationships, personalities, and the positive energy in which life brings. Live holds many great thing.

Life holds many honest answers that sometimes only God can answer. The enemy is always trying to work behind the scenes, behind closed doors to beat you to the punch. The enemy loves to plan the attack to keep you away from the kingdom of God keeping you away from those promises of God. There are sometimes stalled moments that leave you feeling as if you are planted in concrete in which you are not moving.

As a Christian believer be sure to stay away from people that will try to bring you down. A perfect example of this are people who gossip. Gossipers like to tell all of your business. They love to know the juicy details in which they compare their life to the life of others. Gossiping is a poison and it is unhealthy for the kingdom of God.

Proverbs 18:21 says Death and life are in the power of the tongue and they that love it shall eat the fruit thereof. The power of your tongue controls life and death. It's wonderful to know that God has blessed us with a tongue that is so powerful. Powerful enough to control death and life throughout.

1 **Corinthians 2:7** But we speak the wisdom of God in mystery, even the hidden wisdom, which God ordained before the world unto our glory. God says that we speak the wisdom of God. This is the power of wisdom that God gives us. God says we even have access to the hidden wisdom, which God ordained, before the world for his glory. It's important to control our tongues, because of the power that our tongues hold. Remember that death and life are in the power of our tongue.

Gossiping does not help the kingdom of God it only destroys the kingdom of God. It is poison, it is a pollution, and it is no good. You may say well there is such thing as good gossiping. No there is no such thing as good gossiping. Gossiping is wrong and it often leads to talking behind people's backs. If you are not man enough to say it in front of their face then you don't even deserve to talk about it in the first place. When you talk behind someone's back you are weakening your demeanor and you character. You are not man enough to say it in front of their face which makes you weak. It should not even be said in the first place. Like we said before Gossipers only want to know the juicy details. They want to know everything that is happening, when its happening, why its happening, what its happening for, how its happening, where its happening, and who is evolved and for what reasons are the evolved. Talking to friends is okay but gossiping can lead to a big mess. You have to choose your friends carefully and you have to teach others who do not yet know. These individuals are a little naïve or ignorant. There is nothing wrong with the word ignorant. Many individuals few the word ignorant and become offended. Ignorant is simply a lack of not knowing. We all lack knowledge from time to time which is why we must educate ourselves.

In today's fast paced world we live in, we cannot afford to not know. Gossiping is one of the one time playing a team sport can be wrong. Gossiping is often a team sport. Both men and women come together to find our juicy details to the happenings of life. There is nothing wrong with catching up and good times, but when it comes to backstabbing, talking behind peoples backs, using people, and getting over on people that's when things get ugly and that when you need to step aside and let God in. You must beware of your crowd for this affects your breakthrough. Do not get me wrong its important to talk to people, catch up on time that's been lost, and entertain one another as long as its honoring God. When you talk things out you make a good team. You are strengthening your conversation, the way it's handled, and the people you talk to on a daily basis. When talking you know when you have taken it that far. Just don't let it go that far. Be the bigger person and be mature about the situation. Stay away from friends that are going to bring you down, stay away from people that are only going to use you for the details.

Don't be a victim. Don't get used. Be smarter than that. You are smarter than that. You are the bigger person. You are a leader. Remember one must follow in order to lead. It's a proven law. You are a leader! You are a child of the highest God and you are special to God. Gossiping can sometimes go to far. This is when it should be monitored. Your friends should be ones that have your back. Ones that are going to support you through thick and thin. Through the trails and error, throughout the ups and the downs, through peak and valleys and through the mountaintops. Your friends are going to be there to support you. They are going to be there to build you up. They are not their to hurt you but to comfort you and show you the way. To walk with you in alignment and harmony. * God begins to change things in your favor as you continue to be obedient to him. As you do the right things throughout the kingdom you begin to see things align in your favor, to your advantage in which they help you. You will begin to be surprised by the new opportunity that presents itself. Real people do real things and real recognizes real. Its part of your swagger. People will begin to see your style, your swagger, and your attitude. People will begin to respect you. You have to learn to be respectable. You have to first give respect in order to recycle respect throughout life. God continues to work things in your favor. He continues to align breaks in your favor that are part of your breakthrough. God continues to line things up in your favor. God continues, will, and always looks out for you. It's a part of life that God blesses you as you are obedient to him. Breakthroughs bring seasons of change.

Change for new scenery, change for new attitude, change for new people, change for a newness of life. God does not like the same old thing all the time. God loves change and he likes to switch things up from time to time. Its part of the way God handles his business. Its part of change. Continue to do the right thing and be obedient to God and good things will happen to you. God is your friend, your provider, and your mentor. God looks out for you. God has your back and will not let anything happen to you. You might wonder why unfair things happen to good people. There really is no answer for that except to for poor leadership and corrupt governments. Praying, talking to God, and communication with God helps to find these answers. These questions can sometimes not be answered and can only be answered by God at times. This is when it's meant to focus on happier times. Breakthroughs are meant for celebration. Your breakthrough is right around the corner and you can feel it. You can feel the presence, you can feel that mood, you can feel the mode, and you can feel the readiness that comes with your breakthrough.

Your workload continues to increase as you become closer your breakthrough. You have to stay on top of your game. You have to continue to press towards the mark. You cannot slip or afford to slip when deadlines are approaching. Your career is on the line. Beware of individuals that try to come in between your desired goals. These individuals try to hold you back for what God has in store for you because they see your potential. They see your potential and become jealous. They will try to do anything and everything they cab to interferer with your plans.

These individuals you should stay away from for they only get in the way of sound plans. You have to learn how to pace yourself. You have to learn how to work at pace that is comfortable to you but allows you to still get the job done. God continues to bless you as you are faithful to your work. You have to learn how to break down your work. As a Christian believer its important to stay faithful to God, yourself, and the kingdom of God. James 5:16 confess your faults one to another, and pray one for another, that ye may be healed. The effectual fervent prayer of a righteous man availeth much. Fervent prayer availeth much. This means that enthusiasm in prayer is worth of value or profit. As a Christian believer you have to be ready for your breakthrough. Your breakthrough is not going to wait on you. It's not going to fall out the sky.

Its going to take hard work, responsibility, determination, and dedication. Your breakthrough for life is part of your passion for life. Its part of which you are a person. Its what you do as person and what you stand for. As a Christian believer you have to go for your breakthrough. You must have your priorities in line, in tact, and in order. God has new levels of opportunity for you. New avenues, new streets, and new doors for you to walk through. God does not want you to get comfortable, stuck in a rut, and in the same mode all the time. God wants you growing. God wants you to be flexible. Flexible with your schedule, your life, and your career status. You should be ready for what awaits you. We continually talk about God having so much in store for you and its true. God does have big plans for you when you believe. You have to build your believe system up to a new level.

You have to raise above anything that is petty. You have to have a more than conqueror attitude and approach to life. You have to do the right things throughout life. God has new doors for you to walk through. Doors of opportunity that will make you feel good about oneself. Feel good about the way you look, feel good about the way you dress, the way you talk, the way you are seen by people. God is forever making you feel good about yourself. When you feel good about yourself you have a confidence, you have a swag, and you have style about yourself that helps you get through life. Your breakthrough involves people. It involves the collaboration with individuals. You learn to build a confidence within yourself that helps to win through life. A confidence that allows you to feel good about yourself and the life of others.

You also instill a confidence in others that make them feel good, confident, loyal, and trustworthy to you. Your breakthrough is part of your location of what you stand for. It is an iconic historical statue that stand for something. A sense of pride, a sense of ambition, of love, joy, peace, and happiness. Happiness that makes one feel complete. When you come together in collaboration it almost makes everything better. The setting is better, the mood is better, the mode is better, there is less hostility, and life flows to the beat. Life evolves with the seasons. Life begins to flow with the seasons as new thing approach in its due season of what life brings. Breakthroughs happen everyday. They happen to ordinary people, unordinary people, and people from all walks of life. People forms all walks of life experience big breaks everyday. God allows individuals to help you along the way in times that you need it most. God does not see color. God does not see discrimination. God promotes equal opportunity to all walks of life, which is why big breaks happen to anyone.

Again God see's your heart, your intention, and your actions. God see's when people are doing you wrong, people who do not pay attention to you, and people who feel they empower you and take advantage of you. God see's wrongful actions and he is taking accurate note. God is on it. God does not slip. God has an accurate demeanor about him that cannot be touched. As a Christian believer you must learn to complete your tasks. This is part of your follow through in life. Like a pitcher in baseball you must learn to develop an excellent follow through to display strong courage in the competition process of your work. It's important to learn to keep your business to yourself and away from noisy individuals that mean harm. You learn a respect for yourself when you learn to keep your business to yourself.

As a Christian believer, God is your friend, God is your companion. The one you can trust. The one you tell things to. Personal things in which God helps you with in certain situations. Things occur without warning. But God is prepared to mend your troubled heart. This is why you form a close relationship with him. Crime and corruption occur when there is poor leadership and corrupt governments. People do things that try to bring you down and keep you away from your promises of God. This happens when loyal leaders and men of God are not in charge.

You may wonder why nothing you do ever turns out the way you plan. You may wonder why you are depressed, in a daze, or not having any good luck. You have to feel your dreams coming to past. You to feel it in the spirit and you have to see it in the spirit for it to take place. God can make your dreams come to past. One touch of God's favor and you can be thrust to a new level. Writing is a way to release how I feel. It's a way to express one's feelings in a portrayal of what life is. Life holds many great things. Life sometimes let's us down.

Tough things occur, things happen, things go bad in which we did not plan. Things hurt us. We hurt! Of coarse we hurt. And it hurts to hurt. It hurts so deep on the inside. We try to hide the pain. We try to hide the defeat cause we don't want anyone to see us down. But one touch of God's favor, God can turn it around. God see's your heart. God see's your intentions and he see's you. God is arranging things in your favor. Your breakthrough is right around the corner.

CHAPTER 27

Late Register

The true meaning of late registration is those souls that have been saved late in life. Those who have surrendered their life to God at a late point in their life. Late registration is for the people that had a late start in life. Those who have been dealt a bad hand from their own insecurities. Not all have had a late registration in life. Most meet the deadline. Most manage their actual life experiences to avoid late registration. Late registration obviously calls one to receive a late start in life. Late registration comes from one not be prepared for the values that life hold. Life does not what on you. Life does not hand you the cards you always want. You have to be able to make life what you want it. God helps those who want to help their self. Those who want to help the people around you.

God allows you to register late in life, because he has a plan for your life. He knows that there is something greater in store for you throughout the kingdom. God loves you more than you can imagine. We say this constantly again, because it need to be heard.

We often register late in life because we are to caught up in the happenings of the world and what the world has to offer. The world seems so eye-catching to the eye. The world is tempting of the things, which make up the materialistic view of the world.

Sean Maddox

The world will deceive you if you allow it. This is the reason people register late in life is because they have been deceive. God loves you more than you can imagine, which is the reason he sent you into the world temporally for a mission, a purpose.

Late registration is the attitude or approach that you have to life. It's the way you accept life. The way you view life. How life has treated you and how you have treated life. People register late because they have been caught up in the ways of the world. The world offers you the things that you want most. Your most inner desires. The world knows what you want and the world knows that you want it. You are not worried about the happenings of God. You are not worried about living your life for Christ. The first beginning of your life is all about you. How can I live my life? Who can I impress? What more can I gain? These feelings run through your mind as you are living your life. The feelings of God and the plans that he has in store for you are not on your mind at the present moment. When you are not living your life by the word of God or for God, God takes his hand of favor off of you. God's hand of favor protects you from those things in the world. God's hand of favor protects you from the adversary. When we are caught up in those things of the world, we miss the very message God is trying to tell you. You miss the plans that God has in store for you. You are too busy concerning yourself with matters of the world, which are not more important, that God, that you miss the plans that God has in store for you. Everyday that you live, God seeking to build a relationship with you. God is looking for you to carry out the mission or purpose in which he has given you life. We build a relationship with God to know him better. TO know is ways. To know his plans. To know what greater things he has in store for us? It comes with the life given to you that you have a natural ability to know God. To know the plans that God has in store for you.

People who register late in life have had it hard in life. Harder the most others. They do not allow the outcome of the there beginning of their first part of their life to change the destiny towards their success. They do not make excuses for the problems, issues, and outcomes of the situations of their life. When you are late registered you fail to prepare which is the key to success. You can never be to prepared throughout life. The one that is prepared is wise. He listens to God, for the plans that God has in store for him. When you are prepared you have a tamed spirit that waits for the Lord. You do not try to make plans happen on their own. You do not try to lean unto your own understanding. You lean not unto your own understanding.

Proverbs 3:5 (King James Version)
5 Trust in the LORD with all thine heart; and lean not unto thine own understanding.

God ask that you trust in him with all of your heart. He ask that you trust in him always. God allows you to register late because he has something in store for you. You are part of a destiny. You are part of a plan. When you register, you begin a journey in which you are set out to reach your destiny. You set or position yourself in a classroom. On a platform. A stage. A stage that projects the plans of God for the lives that Jesus saved when he was crucified, dead, and buried and he arose on the third day. Jesus blood was shed on the cross for your sins. Jesus blood was shed on the cross for you to come to realization that Jesus died for your sins. Jesus life was sacrificed for you, so that you may have eternal life. The adversary will try to do everything in his power to keep you away from the plans that God has in store for you. The adversary knows how powerful you are when you live accordingly to the plans that God has in store for you. The one that is prepared is the one that wins. The early bird gets the worm.

Surrendering your life to Christ is not about hopping on the bandwagon. It's not about hopping aboard some ship that means nothing to God. Surrendering your life to Christ means everything to God. Whether or not you surrendered your life to Christ early in your life or late, God still loves you the same. The fact that you surrendered your life to Christ is still apart of his plan. God brings you closer to him as you draw closer to him.

Many people who have had a late start in life or registered late in life become some of the most successful people throughout the world. Many high school and college dropouts become some of the most successful multi-millionaires. They do not let the surroundings of their environment keep them from the plans that God has in store for them. God is bigger than the world. God is bigger than man. God has the last say. What God says goes. You can avoid registering late in life by finding God first. When you find God, you draw close to God and find peace within yourself. You find a peace that you never felt before. Knowing that God is there every step of the way. God will never leave you no forsake you.

Hebrews 13:5 (King James Version)
5Let your conversation be without covetousness; and be content with such things as ye have: for he hath said, I will never leave thee, nor forsake thee.

This is the love that Jesus has for you. This is the love that he has for his people. God loves you more than you can even imagine. Beyond your wildest dreams. You are special to God. You belong to part of a seed. A seed that cannot be broken. When God made you, he made you one with him as part of the body of Christ. God will not give you more than you can handle. God gives you what you can handle for a reason, so that you will carry out the will of God. God is looking for those who are obedient to him.

When you register late it is because the adversary has tried to altar the plans that God has in store for you. The adversary does not want you to reach success.

When one registers late in life it requires you to altar your perspective when compared to registering normally in life. The devil tries to keep you away from the plans that God has in store for you. This is the reason why he tries so hard to keep you away from the plans that God has in store for you. God loves you more than you can imagine. God love runs deep. We you are not prepared in life this is where late registration comes into action. Late registration requires you to miss the message that God has in store for you. God relays the message to people who are prepared in life. When you are not prepared this causes you to register late in life. God still does have a plan for you life. God wants to accomplish a goal, a plan, and purpose for your life.

When you are prepared in life you allow yourself to be ready for what life holds. We know that both life and the world has much to offer. God loves you, which is the reason you are apart of his plan. You the ways of lives. You learn the values of life and what life has to offer. Life is what you make it. Life is what you put into it. You get out of life what you put into it. It's that simple. God has given you all that you need to succeed. God allows you to know him more as you grow closer to God. You grow closer to God to receive a better understanding of the plans that God has in store for you. We all learn a different levels. Some more than others, some faster than others. God teaches us the plans that he has in store for us as we draw closer to him. God will not give you more than you can handle. God allows you to know him because he wants to build a relationship with him. As you grow to know God, you grow to know the plans that God has in store for you. God says he will never leave you no forsake you. This is the reason that God will always be there for you. God is there to support you every step of the way. God provides the medicine that you need to get your life back on the right track. No matter how late of a start you have received in life God still loves you. God still has a plan for your life. God is a good God.

CHAPTER 28

Pitfalls, Storms, and Battles

As a Christian believer, we all go through storms. Some more than others. Life almost seems unfair when unfair things happen to good people. God knows how to pull you to another level that allows you to grow with the people around you. God will not give you anything that you cannot handle.

Pitfalls, storms, and battles occur because the adversary knows that God has something great in store for you. We go through storms to become stronger. Many of you are going through storms. Going through issues with your children, divorce, a breakup, drug abuse, alcohol abuse, foreclosure, poverty, health disparity, heart disease, cancer, and abortions. There many different avenues, streets, and pathways that the adversary attempts to attack families. The adversary knows that God has something special in store for you. The adversary knows that God has plan for your life. The is the reason why he attacks so hard. The adversary knows that if he can control your mind he can keep you away from the promises that God has in store for you. He can keep you away from the plans that God has in store for you. There is no greater plan for your life than the plan that God has in store for you. God performs miracles towards all people. No one person is greater than the other. We all do not get there the same way, meaning every person is responsible for his or her own destiny. You control the destiny in which you live. All we are preparing for a greater place. We are preparing for a place that would allow us to have eternal life in the kingdom of heaven. God has allowed you to have eternal life because he loves you.

What is a life without pressure? A life without pressure is a life that is not ordinary. A life that is not real or genuine in the sense that it has not been altered in the sense that the default mechanism has not been fixed to a point that gives you an advantage. The storms that you face in life bring challenges that make you stronger with your walk with the Lord. You become stronger in your faith with God as you face battles in life. The battles we face in life bring casualties at unwanted times. Many of you have lost family members, loved ones, and friends do to personal battles with the adversary. The adversary knows how to strike and he knows when to strike. He hits us where it hurts. He hits us where we it hurts in which it instills pain into our system that does the most damage. Our bodies can only take so much of the adversities of life. Our bodies were designed to prosper and be in health. God says that you will prosper.

3 John 1:2 (King James Version)
2Beloved, I wish above all things that thou mayest prosper and be in health, even as thy soul prospereth.

When God gives you a mission in life, he expects you to complete it. This does not mean that you will not have pitfalls, storms, or battles throughout your lifetime. There are times throughout the kingdom we do not understand. You do not understand that plans that God has in store for you because you have failed to build a covenant relationship with God. When you build a relationship with God, you allow yourself to communicate the plans that God has in store for you. When you face a storm in life, God wants you to know that you do not have to face your battles alone. God is there for you every step of the way. God allows you to go through storms to make you stronger for what he has in store for you next. God is constantly pushing you along. You are child of the highest God.

You may wonder why people are afraid of the Lord or afraid to be saved. They have not become meek enough to receive the spirit of the light from the Lord. The body rejects the light that is shined upon them. When you are not in one accord for the plans that God has in store for you, you cannot receive the message that God has for you. The adversary will try to do everything in his power to keep you away from the plans that God has in store for you. When God starts a work in you, God will complete a work in you. It's a progressive state of mind that evolves as you learn what greater things God has in store for you.

Whatever storms you may be facing, God is there for you every step of the way. God is there to walk you through the battle in which you are facing. God already has the outcome before the battle even starts. He has comeback for every setback that you face. The problem with most people in life is that they have not been patient towards the plans that God has in store for them. They are too busy living their life for the world instead of God. They are too busy playing keeping up with the Jones worrying about what personal wealth they can gain.

You may have come to a point in your life where you feel the world has let you down. Believe me I feel your pain and I see your struggle. I can imagine the pain that you feel after recovering from the lost of a loved one. It comes so unexpected. It comes at a time when your not prepared, when in fact you don't want to be prepared for the lost in which you will face. The adversary strikes at unwanted times and he strikes to enforce pain. I cannot stress enough that you have to know who you are as a person. You have to know that you are a child of the highest God. We say it time and time again that the adversary will try everything in his power to keep you away from the plans that God has in store for you. You have been called out before the foundation of the world. God has called you out for a mission. He knew that he would complete a work in you. A life would not be a life without a storm or battle in which you face. If you are a person that is weak in your faith the adversary will try you. You have to learn to become strong in your faith. The adversary will test you because you are weak. One who learns to master his faith finds his destiny. God has blessed you with a gift in life. Its up to you to use your gift to the best of your advantage. It would be shame to not use the gifts that God has given you. God loves you more than you can imagine. God will not do anything to harm you.

If you are person that has a weak faith, God will bring people in your life that will strengthen your faith. People that will boast you to the next level. People that will help you reach your destiny. God does this because he loves you. Because he trust you. Trust that you will complete a mission that he has instilled in you. God has a way of turning the hands of time around. He has a way of changing things in your favor. You do not have to go through life alone. Many of you are depressed by past experiences that have let you down. Past experiences in which the adversary has attacked you and your family. The adversary strikes when he knows that you are weak. He knows that you cannot control yourself in a weak state of the mind, which is the reason in which he attacks you. He knows that he can control you. Keep you away from God's best. We have to become stronger in our faith. When we are stronger in our faith, we are stronger in our mind. God has given you the power to renew your mind.

When you are feeling down reminisces on the good memories that you have with the Lord and the people you love. God gives us memories to help us get through the tough times. God allows you to remember to make good times. This is the reason why the adversary fights you so hard in your faith. All we see examples of the adversary attacking our families. The adversary knows that we are stronger when we come together which is the reason the adversary tries to isolate you. He tries to keep you away from the people you love. The people that will help you out. The people that will lend a hand to you. The adversary will try to keep you way from the things that you love. He knows that you receive a fulfillment of love that God has to share with you. God shares his love with you because he loves you. There is a satisfaction of love that you receive when you love God.

Pitfalls occur to people who are not prepared. People who have grown away from the Lord. At times there are times in which we become distant from the Lord. This is the reason why we must keep our heads in the bible for the plans that God has in store for us. Working hard towards the plans that God has in store for us is a necessity. It allows us to become mature in the spirit. It's your freewill choice to worship the Lord. God does not force you to worship him. God gives you a choice. You have a calling on your life. Do not be surprised if a storm comes up in your life to prevent you from answering the call or completing the mission in life. God has something greater in store for you. If you do not understand now, soon you will understand. You will understand the ways of the Lord and the plans that God has for you. All that we do for the Lord should be done in the respect of the Lord.

As you become stronger in your faith, you begin to learn to master your faith. You begin to learn more about yourself and what God expects from you. God does not expect a lot from you. He expects for you to live your life in one accord with the plans that he has in store for you. He expects you to become a born again Christian in the sense that you accept Jesus as your Lord and savior.

Sometimes we just don't understand. We don't understand what's expected of us. The adversary loves when we are in this position. He loves to keep us away from the plans that God has in store for us. He loves to keep you confused and in a daze towards to ideas that God has in store for you. This is his way of allowing you to wonder into his kingdom and live in his world for his world instead of living for God. This way he can control and manipulate you into doing the tasks that he has set on his agenda. You might be recovering from an expensive habit. A habit that has thrown you out of the kingdom of God. A habit that has kept you away from the kingdom of God or God's best. You do not have to fall victim to these habits the rest of your life. You have the power to overcome your obstacles. God has given you the power to achieve. God has given you the power to be anything and anybody that you want to be.

Once you learn to find yourself you learn what you are capable of. You learn your limits, the reason in which you were created, the reason in which God has created you. One way to avoid pitfalls is to pay attention to the signs that God is giving you. Are you making new friends? Are you going to church more? In what ways are God blessing you? In what ways has the adversary tried to attack you or your family? These are all important questions in which you should ask yourself. They help you to know the direction in which your life is headed. God has given you a gift for a reason. A gift that you should use to your advantage. God needs for you to use your gifts to the best of your abilities.

Storms come at unwanted time. That strikes at a time when we cannot defend ourselves. The strike our families, the ones that we love the most. You have to know that you love yourself. When you find that you love yourself enough, you find the strength to pull yourself together. You have the power to pull yourself together. Many times we are the only people that understand our own self. It becomes bad to the point that you do not understand yourself. You don't know yourself. You do not know what you have become. You are walking on dangerous ground when this occurs. The adversary tries to keep you away from the things that you love. Possessions that you become attached to. You have to love yourself enough to say that you are going to do something about the situation. God loves you more than you can imagine. Nobody but God himself can explain why unfair things happen to good people. Unfair things happen to good people do to corrupt governments, poor morals, ethics, and leadership. When we do not have Christian people in authority we allow the evilness of the world to come into effect.

The adversary knows that you have dreams of your own. He loves to attack you in the field of your dreams. He knows that if you live your dreams out you will complete the mission in whom God has put in your life. God brings those special people along our path that thrust us to the next level. People that we need. People that we can lean on. These are the people that we can count on through thick and thin. The people we shed tears with. The people we grow to love. The people we love, hug, greet. Remember God has something special for your life. He wouldn't have created you if he did not have something special for you. God needs for you to answer the call. Do not be worried about those things of the adversary. The adversary is simply a distraction trying to keep you away from God's best. You have something special to offer the world. You might be at a point in your life where you feel there is no light at the tunnel. Let me be the one to tell you that there is light at the end of the tunnel. God will not give you a mission that you cannot handle. You are more powerful beyond the measure of which you know that you hold meaning you can accomplish anything that you want in life. We are often too impatient to answer that call that God has in store for us. God has given you a gift for a reason to complete a mission in you for a purpose. Its up to you to complete that mission. The sooner you find out your calling in life the sooner you can complete your mission in life. God needs for you to live your life to the utmost. Live your life with honor, pride, and authority. You hold the power to take authority of your life. God is a good God.

CHAPTER 29

Mastering Your Faith

As a Christian believer you hold the power to master your faith. You hold the power to control your destiny. The covenant you have with God is part of an incorruptible seed that cannot be broken. God has a plan for your life and it all starts with you. The faith that you have for yourself is determined by the way that you live your life.

All Satan has attempted to deceive you from the plans that God has in store for you. Satan tempted Adam and Eve in the garden. Satan said thou shalt not surely die.

Genesis 3:3 (King James Version)
3But of the fruit of the tree, which is in the midst of the garden, God, hath said, ye shall not eat of it, neither shall ye touch it, lest ye die.

Genesis 3:4 (King James Version)
4And the serpent said unto the woman, ye shall not surely die:

Satan attempted to change the words of God saying that you should not surely die. Satan knows the power that your faith holds. He knows the power that you hold as a human being. Your faith has the power to move mountains. God only ask that you have faith the grain of a mustard seed.

Matthew 17:20 (King James Version)
20And Jesus said unto them, Because of your unbelief: for verily I say unto you, If ye have faith as a grain of mustard seed, ye shall say unto this mountain, Remove hence to yonder place; and it shall remove; and nothing shall be impossible unto you.

It doesn't take much for God to accomplish the plans that he has in store for you. God only ask that you believe in him. Believe his ways. Believe that all things are possible. All things are made possible with the faith that you have that comes from within through life. God gives you faith so that you may believe. When you have no faith, you have no believe. You cannot set out to accomplish the dreams, goals, ambitions, and aspirations that you have for yourself. When you live a life without goals, you live a life that cannot prevail. The goals that you set for yourself define yourself and the future that you hold.

God knows the ways of the adversary. He knows that the adversary is out to sell your soul. You hold something special on the inside of you. A seed that belongs to the body of Christ. The seed enables you to grow through the spirit for the plans that God has in store for you. The seed that you have is part of your faith. It's a part of the plan that God has in store for you. We talk a lot about the plans that God has in store for you because they are important. You are important to God. You may not feel important, but you are. God loves you. God will never leave you no forsake you. God is here for you every step of the way. There are certain things in life that you cannot take on alone. God allows you to study and dissect his word to know him more. Through your faith, God will speak to you. God will tell you the plans that he has in store for you. Maybe God's plans are for you to be a doctor; maybe God's plans are for you to be a minister.

Whatever the plans may be, its all a part of God's master plan for all of mankind to have eternal life.

Your faith is mastered through practicing God's word on a daily basis. Maybe you are suffering from a strong addiction of drugs or cigarettes. God can help you quit the habit. You do not have to become a slave to adversary. You do not have to carry out the plans of the devil. You can live free from the sin. The adversary loves to persuade you to sin. We know that the wages of sin is death.

Romans 6:23 (King James Version)
23For the wages of sin is death; but the gift of God is eternal life through Jesus Christ our Lord.

When you continue to sin you are destroying the faith that you have through God. You are allowing your life to come to an end. This is the way the adversary tries to kill you. The adversary knows that God has a plan for your life, which is why he works so hard to defeat. God knows you heart. God knows the intentions, actions, and believes that you hold within. You hold these believe from within, because you are displaying the love that you have for God. In return, God shows his mercy upon you. God rewards those who seek after him.

Hebrews 11:6 (King James Version)
6But without faith it is impossible to please him: for he that cometh to God must believe that he is, and that he is a rewarded of them that diligently seek him.

When you seek God, you allow your spirit to become mature through faith. You ignore those things that are not of the kingdom of God, because you have matured past those things that are foolish. You focus on situations, events, and outcomes that are pleasing to God. Your faith is seeking to please the Lord and his works. You became part of the body of Christ the second you accepted Jesus as your Lord and savior.

The adversary will do many things to true to altar your faith. He will try to keep you from God's best. When you are matured in the spirit you ignore those things of the adversary. The new events, situations, and happenings of life allow you the chance to test your faith. There are many tests in life. Test to promote to the next level for what is greater in store for you. Your faith allows you to prepare for this test. Your faith holds the power to thrust you to the next level of life. We are all seeking a next level opportunity that allows us to show the faith that we hold. The adversary will test your faith. When you are weak in the spirit you hold a better chance of altering the plans that God has in store for you. This is why you must draw close to God.

James 4:8 (King James Version)
8Draw nigh to God, and he will draw nigh to you. Cleanse your hands, ye sinners; and purify your hearts, ye double minded.

You draw close to God to know him more. To learn his ways. To learn what he has in store for you. Your faith is determined by what it is that you believe in. What is it that you believe in? What moves you? What allows you to know God more? What allows you to practice you faith. You have been equipped with the power of all mighty God. God has something greater in store for you, which is the reason he constantly reminds you. When you do not believe you limit your faith. You limit the powers that you hold within to allow you to reach your goals. Your faith is built through believing. You believe in the body of Christ. You believe that Jesus died for your sins.

Hebrews 11:1 (King James Version)
1Now faith is the substance of things hoped for, the evidence of things not seen.

When you first begin to master your faith you cannot focus on not making mistakes in life. Everyone makes mistakes. No one who ever walked God's green earth his not made a mistake. Your main focus should be to become pleasing to God. TO live your life to the plans that God has in store for you. In the world you don't often see much faith. People are often negative all the time. This negativity ruins the you becoming God's best. In order to please God, you have to have faith. Your faith will grow as you become confident in his word. God allows you to know him more as you grow closer to him. You know God more through reading the bible. This is part of your faith. The bible is the blueprint for your life. It holds all the answers to life. The bible is the most central piece of literature written. It guides you through the problems, issues, and obstacles that you face in life. You cannot go at life alone you need the help of all mighty God. When you discover the love that God has for you, it is hard not live a life that is pleasing to God.

Learning the ways of the world is not the way to master your faith. God needs you to draw closer to him and he will draw closer to you. Many people have been left in the dark because they have not taken the time to draw closer to God. They have not taken to the time to learn the ways of God and all that God has in store for them. You defeat the adversary by keeping your head in the word of God. By knowing God's principals. By knows the plans that God has in store for you. You cannot know the plans that God has in store for you when you do not know God. This is the reason that we draw closer to God.

Your faith is determined by what you believe. What is it that you believe? How are you living your life for God? When you are to busy listening to those things of the world you cannot hear from God. You cannot hear the plans that God has in store for you. You cannot practice those things that will harm your faith. You cannot commit yourself to sin and the ways of this world. The ways of this world look good to the eye. They seem as if they are a way you will know forever. Remember this life is temporary. God has something greater in store for you. God has a plan for your life.

Sean Maddox

Many people become upset because they do not see their plans coming to past fast enough. They give up on the plans that God has in store for them because they do not see their plans coming to past fast enough. This occurs through one having a weak faith. One loses the believe that he has for the things around them. You must learn to have a stronger faith when those things are not coming to past. You could risk the chance of attempting to live a life that is not destined for you. You cannot fall into the rut of failure of trying to live someone else's life. You are not that person. If God wanted you to be that person, he would have created you that way.

Why do we compare ourselves to others? We compare ourselves to others because we feel less about ourselves. We feel less about the way that God created us to be. We wish we had more. The want that you have always desires more of what the world has to offer. We know that the world offers a lot. You can still obtain the things that you want out of life and show your love for God in the same way. You do not have to sell your soul to the devil to receive the things that you want most out of life. God brings those people along your path that are special to both you and him. People that will strengthen your faith. People that will draw you closer to the kingdom of God. You do not want to hang around people that are going to pull you away from God. These people have been left in the dark and cannot see the light that shines through the words because they are not saved.

You hold the power to control your future. Do not worry about what others may say about you. The adversary sends people who are jealous of you who try to keep you away from God's best. You should insure yourself that you are living your life to the best of your ability. This insures that you will master the faith that you put into the universe. Do not allow anyone to control your life. People often try to control another person life because they feel less about themselves. God has great things in store for you. God is awesome good.

CHAPTER 30

Destiny

Your destiny is a fixed order or scenarios of your natural outcome of what the future may hold for you.

As a Christian believer, you hold the power to control you destiny. Your destiny is what you make it. Many people believe there destiny is where they end up. How they will turn out. What there income or status will become. This is all true, but your destiny is more than that. Your destiny is a part of God. It's the decisions that you make throughout life. How are you treating yourself? What criteria are you saying about yourself? Where do you feel you will end up in the years to come? How has your destiny turned out in the past? Has it been everything that you expected or more? Many people have not taking control of their destiny because they have not taken control of themselves. When you control yourself, you allow yourself self-control over your future and what it may hold for you in the years to come. You have to guard yourself, the people around you, and your future. What people are you associating yourself with? In what ways are you affiliated? How do you view your self? If you cannot tell when finding yourself or taking control of your destiny many questions come into factor for the plans that you have for yourself, but most importantly the plans that God has in store for you.

Maybe you are a person that has failed in the past. Maybe your life has not turned out the way that you want it you do not have to live in defeat. You do not have to play into the adversary hands. You hold the power to control your destiny. Your destiny is determined by the decisions that you make. Whether right or wrong in your decisions making process you control your future. Specific aspects and criteria in life affect us all. The decisions that you make up your life. This is the reason many people play the games of chess or checkers. Chess and checkers are filled with important decisions making skills. People take the time to hone their skills to the many aspects, turns, and curve balls that life throws as them. You might feel that you are getting older in life and there are certain decisions, accomplishments, and goals that you would like to see yourself accomplish throughout life. You should feel this way. You should never come to a point in your life where you feel that there isn't anything else in which you want to accomplish. This is known as a dangerous situation. This is dangerous to your life, your health, and the decisions that you are putting forth on a daily basis. As a Christian believer you want to continue to grow in the fruit of the spirit throughout life. You want everything that life has to offer. Life has many different various options, choices, and avenues to offer you when you begin to take control of your life. Do you want a better job, a promotion, more money, a family, a husband, a wife, or happiness? Whatever the decision may be you the power to control your life. Do not give anyone the opportunity to control your destiny. Your life was given to you and no one else. You have the power to be free.

Certain sacrifices are needed as leverage to control the destiny in which you seek out to achieve in life. You should never be confused about what your destiny may hold for you. Reasons of being confused would be the cause of the result of not knowing yourself first and foremost. Knowing yourself and what your capable of is essential throughout life. You should know where it is you want to see yourself in the next five years. Where do you plan to live? What type of job or industry do you plan to work in? How can you help the people around you reach their goals towards their destiny? These are all questions that come into hand when reaching your goals towards your destiny. What plans or goals do your have for your children? In the bible it says that we should leave an inheritance for our children's, children.

Proverbs 13:22 (King James Version)
22A good man loveth an inheritance to his children's children: and the wealth of the sinner is laid up for the just.

God plans for the future. God looks out for the future. He looks out for those who are to come in the near future. Here is a command for God for the plans that God has in store for us to live our life out in the likeness of Christ.

Every decision you make controls your destiny. It controls the actions, the plans, and the goals you plan to reach. Whether positive or negative in you is decision-making process matters. Your decisions affect your future. It affects the people around you. Remember you hold the power to control your future. Control your financial future, your destiny, success, failures, setbacks, and comebacks. Every setback is an opportunity for a comeback. You do not have to live in defeat. You do not have to play into the adversary hands. God has a plan for your life and it all starts with you. You have to be prepared throughout life. Preparation is the key. When you are prepared you are equipped. You live your life in victory. You are the victor and not the victim. Everything in life happens for a reason. The occurrences that happen to you in life are real. They happen to promote you to the next level. You never want to get stuck in a rut. You have the power to control your future. Your future is full of power. Full of choices. Full of decisions. Decisions that affect your future for the better or the worse. You have to learn to mix the good with the bad, but take it all with a grain of salt. This book is written to motivate you to find yourself in life. Many people are lost in their life. In life people stray off coarse for the plans that God has in store for them. People get lost on their journey to their destiny. You end up listening to false Gods, false prophets, and adversaries. You buy in to what they are saying rather than believing God. This is what happens when you believe what man says rather than what God says. God knows what's best for you. God knows you better than anyone else.

As a Christian believer, you have to stay focus. To many times we lose focus on the plans and goals that we have set for ourselves. We allow the distractions of the world to altar the plans that we have set for you along with the plans that God has set for us. Maintaining focus will set the tone for the accomplishments that you achieve throughout life. You stay focused by keeping your mind in the word of God. We study to show you approved unto God.

2 Timothy 2:15 (King James Version)
15Study to show you approved unto God, a workman that needed not to be ashamed, rightly dividing the word of truth.

When you study the word of God you discover the plans that God has in store for you. God plans for you written throughout the bible. God promises to deliver on his promises. God is not false, he is not fake, and he is real, authentic, and pure. Keeping a pure heart is needed to hear the plans that God has in store for you. When you have a pure heart you have a holy heart. You can hear from the plans that he is communicating to you throughout life. You might not feel that God has a plan for you in your life. You are special to God. You are part of a greater plan. God does have a plan for your life. Here is a promise from God that explains the plans that God has for you.

Jeremiah 29:11 (King James Version)
11For I know the thoughts that I think toward you, smith the LORD, thoughts of peace, and not of evil, to give you an expected end.

God already knows the plans that he thinks of you. God plans are ones that come with peace and not evil that will give you a promising future. Do not get discouraged if you have not achieved the level of success that you will like to achieve, your day is coming. God will complete a good work in you.

Your future holds the plans that you set for it. The goals that you set out to achieve are up to what you are feeding your mind. You cannot control the future, but you can plan for it. As you plan for the future you can arrange yourself in a manner that allows you to set yourself up for positive outcomes in your destiny.

God begins to move or arrange things in your favor throughout life. You do not have to chase your destiny in which you may have felt in the past was far fetched. Your destiny is right in front of you. You simply have to reach out and grab it.

Your destiny can be inevitable and unchangeable in which the different courses of action people take may still lead to a predetermined destiny in heaven. This may or may not be true, for no one truly knows his or her destiny except among earth.

We often talk about the importance of our state of mind. When you learn to control your state of mind, you learn to control the person you are, grow to be, and will soon become throughout life. You can control your future with your thoughts. When you control how you think, you control who you are as a person. Do not allow anyone to have control over your thoughts and how you may feel. This can be very personal to you and the people around you.

When you discover the power that you destiny holds you begin to appreciate it more. You begin to discover the reason for your existence the person you are, and the person that you will become. You control who you are as a person throughout life by controlling yourself. Control your thoughts; control your actions, your beliefs, your religion, facts, truths, family, career status, and situational outcomes in life.

Your destiny is arranged off a set of ideas. This is why it is so important to control your thinking. Control the signals that you are putting out into the universe as we learned in the chapter titled "Making your thoughts a reality".

Many people try to control their destiny and do not know how. When you learn the power of your thoughts you learn the power you hold to control your destiny. Every thought that you think is one that is aimed at your destiny. One that makes up a career status of events that put the pieces of the puzzle of your destiny together. Your destiny is what you make it. It's how you treat your life. What are you saying about yourself? What are saying about your future? How are you taking car of you? How are you arranging things in your favor? God is continuing to arrange things in your favor. When you learn to control the power of your thoughts, you learn to control your future. You can break down the power of your past thoughts to help to control your future. Examine your past. Where has it taken you? What roads, avenues, and streets did you take? Where did they lead you? What did they mean to you? How can change things in your future that you did not like about your past? What events in your past have held you back? What events have left scars? Scars from wars, scars from battles, scars for fights you were forces to fight with the adversary. How has the adversary tried to take control of your destiny or life? In what ways has God protected you from the adversary? In what ways have you protected yourself from the adversary? The adversary comes to kill, steal, and to destroy.

Now that you control your thoughts you now hold the power to direct your future. You hold the power to control what your future may hold or bring. Your destiny can bring you good fortune, happiness, family, sorrow, pain, depression, or misery. You might be thinking why would you want to bring sorrow, pain, depression or misery? You might not want to bring it, but it is all factored in to the realities of life that it still exists. We know that the universe responds to our thoughts through brain signals that we are putting out into the world. You hold the power to control those thoughts. You cannot and will not reach your destiny alone. It is one that is traveled as a team effort at times. One that is both lonely and not lonely.

Your brain begins to think of things that you want. Things that make you happy. The way that you want to see yourself in the near future. The universe then responds to the best situation or scenarios that will make up the destiny that are apart of Gods plans for you. You are part of bigger destiny set apart from simply yourself. Life is not all about you! There is more to life than just you. You are part of a bigger plan. Part of God's plan. The plans that God has in store for you are always greater than your own throughout the world. Begin to see yourself as part of the plans that God has in store for you instead of the plans that you have in store for yourself and all the pieces of the puzzle will begin to take place. Avoid thinking negative thoughts about yourself and others to avoid those vibration signals in which you send out to the universe. You do not want the universe responding to negativity. This is not to say that it will not happen, because negativity is a reality in which it will occur. However you do hold the power to your destiny to control the thoughts that occur in your life. You hold the power to control your thoughts. God is good God.

CHAPTER 31

Legendary

The truth is you are too real for society. You are in a league of your own. God has a plan for your life. You have a natural business sense. You were born with it. It's part of genes in which God has developed with in you. Its natural sense of God given talent that lays within you. No one can take away the talent in which God has in trust for you. You reach legendary status with the help of God. Legendary status is not handed to you. It is not given to you. It is one that is earned. It is one that affects you and the people around you. God needs for you to apply the principals of his word that God has laid out for you throughout life. Everywhere you look people are working hard. Working hard for the things that they want out of life. Some people reach their breakthrough faster than others. It all happens when God wants it to happen. It's all-apart of Gods plan. We learned in the chapter about patience that God has plan for your life. We know that is happens when God wants it to happen. To become a legend in life you achieve that status through patience. You achieve that status by not rushing a creation is which God is creating on the inside of you. God's light shine through you into the kingdom of God in which helps to illuminate the world.

Legendary status comes from not being known. It comes from being unknown and the world. We know that all legends were once a nobody throughout life. They started out with nothing and made something doing what God created them to do. This is the importance of finding what it is that God created you to do. We know that millions of people are in a field that they are unhappy with. A field that limits their productivity to the advancement of their career throughout life. You cannot do it by yourself. You have to do it with the help of God throughout life. God has called you out before the foundation of the world. God has start a work in you that he will complete in the process of creativity for the workmanship for the kingdom of God.

Legends are born. Legends are created. They walk with pride. They hold their head up. Legends don't panic during times of trials and tribulations. They overcome danger, adversity, and obstacles. Many obstacles will come your way, but you have to be ready for them. DO spend your time being somebody that your not. Be the person that God created you to be throughout life. A legend is when that is clean, presentable in the spirit and one that has overcome obstacles in life that had plans to set one back. A legend has sacrificed many endeavors that have once been presented to set one back, but have been overcome with the help of God. A legend is polite to the people around them. A legend has emulated the people around them to the perfection of ones demeanor that allows one to stand out in the temple of God. A legend is one with pride. One who is powerful and one who does not abuse its power. A legend obeys the commandments of God and leads by example. A legend works towards his goals. A legend has a plan at all times and is rarely seen without one. A legend sees and conquerors those tasks that life throws at him. A legend has something to offer the world and the people around them by making them better by simply being himself. A legend is pure. A legend keeps a pure soul. A legend is ready for battle at times that battle has not yet struck. A legend is prepared. A legend is classy and carries him in way that is leading to the example of the people around him. A legend is rarely confused. A legend has a clear path for the plans that God has laid out for him throughout life. A legend has a team of advisors. When you are legendary you listen to the people around and make choices that go accordingly to Gods principals. A legend uses the legendary status of the people around him. A legend makes history. A legend surrounds himself with legendary people. Legendary people walk with pride. They hold their head up. Its part of the late bloomer. Its part of the most in which God has created on the inside of you. A legend is an overcomer. A legend works hard at his craft.

You are legendary. You have something to offer the world. You are part of a new movement whose goals are to save lives, inspire others, and lead by example. A legend demands his respect. A legend continues to carry him with pride. A legend doesn't try to get over on someone. This is the morals, ethics, and respect that a legend has for the people around him. A legend watches his back. A legend has many enemies who have not taken the time to master their faith in which they hate on the success of the outcomes of the blessings that God has blessed him with. A legend is cunning in the sense that he is clever to the touch. A legend is quick on his toes. Legends come in all different sizes shapes, colors, textures, and textiles. A legend is a moneymaker. A legend attracts money. A legend hustles for the things that he wants out of life. A legend doesn't waste time. A legend is a God given gift! Legendary people have an affect on people. Legendary people make mistakes like anyone else. Legendary people learn from their mistakes. Legendary people love their family. They listen to God and the plans that God has in store for them. Legend people are like a magnet they attract people to them that help them to achieve their goals. Legendary people have swag. They have style. They carry themselves with respect and they receive respect from others. Legendary people spread the word of God. Legendary people talk about plans that will take them to another level.

Legendary people enjoy the fruits of their labors. Legendary people take nothing and make something. They work out, they keep themselves up. Legendary people have a pride and respect that others do not. Legendary people know their destination. They pick up the load when others slack. Legendary people never make excuses for their mistakes. They learn from others who laid the footprints before them. Legendary people are hard to find. They are career driven. Legend people are kings. They start new trends. They make people want to be like them. Legends make decisions that go accordingly to the plans of their life. Legendary people move quickly. Their quick on their toes. They use what God has given them to advance the kingdom of God. They use their talents to the best of their abilities and focus on their strengths rather than their weaknesses.

Legends don't get mad, they figure things out. They are always busy in the sense they always have something to do. They are simple minded and do not complicate things. They appreciate the simple things in life. Legends are moneymaking machines. Legends understand that you only live once. Legends illuminate life. They help people when they are down. Legends don't think of themselves as better than everyone else. People who think that they think that they are better than everyone else don't understand the true principals in life. They don't understand that legends work hard to achieve the level of success that they have achieved. Legends think of themselves as good. They think of themselves as productive. Legends live on forever. They work hard for the things that they want out of life. Legends move with swag. They have a wonderful business sense about them. People love to be around them. They rarely run out of ideas. They keep pushing to be all that they can be. Legends are their own army. Their own battalion, their own company. Legends make things happen. Legends don't lie, cheat, and steal to make things happen. Legends have many close friends. Legends are rarely confused. Legends wait for Jesus' return. They lead by example and they know right from wrong. Legends play their cards right. They play the hand that was dealt to them. Legends don't make excuses. Legends don't sweat the small stuff. They know that Jesus has died for them and Jesus will return to take them up to heaven. Legends are champions. The people around them love them. They work hard for the things that they want out of life. Legends have been defeated. Legends have had downfalls pitfalls, storms, and battles. Legends always have respect for others. They do what's necessary for their survival.

Legends are creative. They use the creativity that God has given them to better themselves. Legends don't waste time. A legend doesn't run when the devil strikes. A legend stands up to his own problems. A legend keeps silent at times that are needed. A legend worships God. A legend hustles hard. A legend raises hell. A legend soars to new levels. A legend finds what works for him. A legend does not worry about keeping up with the Jones. A legend has independent. A legend has mastered his career status. A legend has made many mistakes. A legend is career driven. A legend is one who does not lose hope. A legend doesn't worry about whether or not he cannot get the job done. A legend walks with pride. A legend feels good to be back. A legend has had relationships with many women. Women he trusts. Women as friends. Women as partners. Partners in faith and partners in crime. Legends have no boundaries. Legends handle their business. A legend dresses for success and is clean in appearance.

As a Christian believer, you can reach legendary status through hard work. God has something special for your life. God has something great in store for you. You have to believe that God has something great in store for you. Once you stop believing, you have a problem. You lose your faith. You lose everything that God is working within you. God is continuing to do a good work within you. When you are legendary, you feel good about yourself. You feel good about the people around you. God continues to pour his love out for you and the people around you as you are faithful to him.

To become legendary you must have dedication. You must be dedicated to your craft.

Ambition comes with the status of being legendary. Leave all those things in the past behind. They try to hold you down. They try to keep you away from the plans that God has in store for you.

You grow closer to God through ambition. You begin to build the lasting relationship with God that we are talking about. Your family and friends love you. This is part of becoming a legend. You find that people around you truly care for you. People want to see you do well throughout life.

Your swag plays a major part of you becoming a legend. It helps to define who bayou are as a person throughout life. God is a good God throughout life. God has so much in store for you when you believe. You are an overcomer. Any person who has achieved legendary status has become an overcomer in their lifetime. People are looking for people who are real. People who are genuine. People who are authentic in life. People that you can trust.

You reach a certain career status when you become legendary. You become thrust to a new level. A level of uncertainty. A level of certainty. Becoming a legend has a certain amount of pressure on oneself. You begin to deal with new endeavors, challenges, and changes you once did not take on before you become a legend. Your life now changes. You become changed for the better. You change into the mold that God is now preparing you for. Old things will not matter as much as you are now being transformed into the likeness of God. Everything happens in its due season. You are being molded by the season into the plans that God has in store for you.

I wrote this chapter to help you find the legend in you. You can read the words on these pages from all these books and find criteria in which you can relate because you to are legendary. You are part of a creation from God. A mission a purpose. You to can become a legend in due time. Its takes hard work determination and motivation. You can reach legendary status with Gods help. To become legendary you must do the things that God created you for. You are wondering why are not receiving results because you are to busy trying to be something that your not! Simply be yourself and become one with God.

CHAPTER 32

Surrendering Your Life To Christ

As a Christian believer, you hold the power to surrender your life to Christ. You hold the power to save your soul. You may be a person that does not know Christ. You may have went through your whole life and not surrender to the plans that God has in store for you. Maybe God has brought you to that certain point in life. A point that allows you to wake up to the realization that Jesus is your Lord and savior. Jesus died for your sins, so that you may have eternal life. This means that you will live on forever in the kingdom of heaven. Once you are saved, no one holds the power to take your life away. You belong to God. You belong to the kingdom of God. God's plans for you are to have eternal life.

Before you surrendered your life to Christ, you lived your life in defeat. The adversary took control of your life and the plans that God had in store for you. The adversary controlled you. God has given you the power to have dominion over your life. Over your future. When you surrender your life to Christ you become one with God and one with Christ. Jesus loves you enough to sacrifice his life for the life of mankind. Jesus listened to God when to Jesus throughout the kingdom God instructed him to be crucified on the cross. Jesus was crucified, dead, and buried. On the third day he arose from the dead. This is the new body in which Christ gave of God. God loved you enough to give his life for yours.

When you surrender your life to Christ you live above the curse. Above the curse of poverty, defeat, and the adversary. The adversary will do everything in his power to sell your soul, but you will not when you believe that Jesus had died for your sins. Jesus life was given for you so that you might have eternal life. Eternal life is part of the plan that God has in store for you.

Before you had eternal life, you lived your life to the world's standards. You were of this world. You were put in this world, but not of this world.

John 15:19 (King James Version)
19If ye were of the world, the world would love his own: but because ye are not of the world, but I have chosen you out of the world, therefore the world hatter you.

The world hatter you because the world does not understand you. You are saved through Christ. There are millions of people throughout the world who are not saved. They do not understand your ways because they have not been saved through Christ. They do not hold the spiritual intelligence that a Christian has. When you are saved you come to understand of what Christ has done for you. You also live in a spiritual realm. You belong to God. You understand his ways. The spiritual intelligence that you hold allows you to live your life in victory. It allows you to know the plans that God has in store for you. We know that God sent us here to save lives so that all souls may go to the kingdom of heaven. God wants all lives to enter the kingdom of heaven and they will with your help. Remember John 3:16 and Romans 10:9 allow you to save lives

When you surrender your life to Christ it requires you to live your life for Christ. This means that you are Christ like. You live your life to Christ in everyway. You take on actions and plans that God has created for you to fulfill through a mission or purpose in life. Before you surrendered your life to Christ you did not know the ways of God. This is seen as you compare your life to the way it was displayed compared to the way you now live with Christ. You surrender your life to Christ so that you will not live your life for the adversary.

When you surrender your life to Christ, God begins to tell you the plans that he has in store for you. He tells you your gifts, what you are good at, what you will become, how you will live your life, how others will view you. This all happens as you live your life for God. God knows that the enemy is after you, which is why he sent his son to save you from the world. This is why you believe that Jesus has died for your sins. Jesus died so that you might be saved. You are saved because you believe. You believe what Christ has done for you. You believe that you will have eternal life. You believe that Jesus died for you.

If you are wondering why your life did not come to pass in the past its because you were not saved. You were living you life for the world instead of God. Remember we are not of this world. We were sent here temporarily for a mission and direct purpose to serve God. You are servants of God. There is great reward in service. This is why so many business offer their services. These business also operate off of God's principals. Businesses operate off of principals according to the bible.

Surrendering your life to Christ requires you to believe that Jesus died for you. He died that you might have life and have it eternal. God's love for you stretches out further than you can imagine. This is the reason he allows Jesus to die for you, so that you may live free from sin.

When you surrender your life to Christ it becomes part of an incorruptible seed that cannot be broken. Your life belongs to both God and Jesus. This is why we must always pray to God through Jesus Christ. No one comes to the father, but through Christ.

John 14:16 (King James Version)
16And I will pray the Father, and he shall give you another Comforter, that he may abide with you for ever;

This is the respect that you must have for Christ and must have for you. Imagine what kind of life you would live if you did not surrender your life to Christ. You would live a life full of sin. The only difference between the sin that you commit when your are saved from the sin that you commit when you are not saved is the sin that you commit when you are not saved will not be forgiven. This means that you will have to pay for the sin that you commit. God has cast your sin out as far as the east is from the west. God allows you to be forgiven, because he loves you. When you believe that you are saved. You are saved through Christ.

Jesus listened through obedience when he was told to surrender his life to God. I reward Jesus became the person that saved the lives of all mankind. What a powerful statement that moves mountains. The love that you have for both God and Jesus is proved through the life that you a choose to live. Surrendering your life to Christ gives you life. It gives you eternal life. Life so that you may live forever. God loves you enough to send his only son to save your life. In return you should surrender your life to Christ.

If you are person that has not surrendered their life to Christ, I would personally love to give you the chance. What a great reward for agreeing to live our life for Christ. Both John 3:16 and Romans 10:9 allow you to surrender your life to Christ so that you might have eternal life. Below we have listed both scriptures so that you may recite now in which you will become saved. What amazing power Jesus has for you. When you recite these two scriptures you are saving your life. You are living above the curse. Your life now becomes a part of the plans that God has in store for you.

John 3:16 (King James Version)
16For God so loved the world that he gave his only begotten Son, that whosoever believeth in him should not perish, but have everlasting life.

Sean Maddox

Romans 10:9 (King James Version)
9That if thou shalt confess with thy mouth the Lord Jesus, and shalt believe in thine heart that God hath raised him from the dead, thou shalt be saved.

You may be a person that has not known God. You may have been living you life for the adversary, which is the reason you have had so much trouble in your past. The adversary makes you believe that you are living your life for God, but you are truly living your life for him. God is looking to know you more. God is looking to build a relationship with you.

When you surrender your life to Christ you immediately become free of the bondage of the adversary. God sets you free from the prison you were once held in through a spiritual realm. You now become one with Christ in which your life becomes in alignment and harmony with the plans that God has in store for you.

God allows the free will choice whether to believe in him or not. It is not a require that you believe in God. God does not force you to believe his word. Most people do. They believe the many promises that are held within God's word. They believe what Jesus has done for them. They believe in the power of saving lives. They believe that Jesus will soon return so that we all may go to heaven. This is all apart of surrendering your life to Christ. Remember it is part of sacrifice that we have made. Jesus ascribed his life for you so that you may have eternal life. This may be all new to you, but this is the love that Jesus has for you. You love yourself when you love God. Remember Jesus died so that you may have eternal life. God is a good God.

CHAPTER 33

Jesus's Return

As a part of God's plan for the kingdom of God, Jesus will return. Jesus is coming back for you in which you will have eternal life and live in heaven. It's all a part of God's master plan. As a Christian believer, you want to be prepared for the return of Jesus. Jesus will come for you as promised. To be prepared for Jesus return, are you living your life in the eyes of God in a Christ like way? Are living with honor, respect, discipline, and morals. Jesus is seeking to show favor in these that are living by his word. Those who read his word. Those who know his word. The end is coming soon. Sooner than you think.

Matthew 24:14 (King James Version)
14And this gospel of the kingdom shall be preached in all the world for a witness unto all nations; and then shall the end come.

The gospel is preached to billions of people throughout the world. Billions of people know God. They are drawing closer to God from the unwanted evil ways of the world. The bible says the end shall come after the gospel of the kingdom of God is preached for the world to witness unto all nations. Today we are witnesses the gospel of the world more and more. More and more people are surrendering there live to Christ. They are giving their life to Christ. They are preparing for Jesus return. They are preparing for the resurrection of life. You prepare yourself for the return of Jesus by first surrendering your life to Christ. When you surrender your life to Christ you are now saved. You are now free from the sin in which you commit. You now have a seed that cannot be broken. There isn't anything that anyone can do to take that seed away from you.

Matthew 24:4 (King James Version)
4And Jesus answered and said unto him, Take heed that no man deceive you.

Matthew 24:5 (King James Version)
5For many shall come in my name, saying, I am Christ; and shall deceive many.

You must be sure that man does not deceive you. Many will come in the name of Jesus to deceive the world. Satan tries to discuss himself as Christ. He tries to come in the name of Jesus. The world is filled with many adversary. People, places, and things that are not prepared for Jesus return. People that live their life to the world's standards instead of Jesus. God helps you along the way. He says your requests, actions, and efforts provides the help that you need to allow you to reach your destiny. Your real destiny is heaven. This is your ultimate goal. We are all living our life to reach heaven. Some say you reach heaven by one living a good life. This statement remains true. God is looking for Christian people. People that live their life according to God and not the world.

Matthew 24:6 (King James Version)
6And ye shall hear of wars and rumors of wars: see that ye be not troubled: for all these things must come to pass, but the end is not yet.

The world will fight within itself because the world does not understand one another. People are not taking the time to understand one another. Understand where another is coming from. There are gaps that need to be filled in order for the world to come together. The world is such a powerful creation, it has so much to offer. God said the end will not yet come during the trials and tribulations of these wars. The world must come together as one body in Christ believing in God before Jesus will return. You hold the power to make this happen through your believing. It's all apart of your faith. You must take the time to master your faith. Your master your faith through building a relationship with God.

Hell is no place anyone wants to go. It's an kingdom of the adversary. People who are not prepared for Christ risk the chance of their destiny taking them to hell.

Matthew 24:29 (King James Version)
29Immediately after the tribulation of those days shall the sun be darkened, and the moon shall not give her light, and the stars shall fall from heaven, and the powers of the heavens shall be shaken:

Revelation 16:18
18And there were voices, and thunders, and lightnings; and there was a great earthquake, such as was not since men were upon the earth, so mighty an earthquake, and so great.

Revelation 16:19 (King James Version)
19And the great city was divided into three parts, and the cities of the nations fell: and great Babylon came in remembrance before God, to give unto her the cup of the wine of the fierceness of his wrath.

Matthew 24:30 (King James Version)
30And then shall appear the sign of the Son of man in heaven: and then shall all the tribes of the earth mourn, and they shall

see the Son of man coming in the clouds of heaven with power and great glory.

This is the sign of Jesus return. Jesus will come as a sign as the son of man in heaven. We shall then see the son of man coming to the clouds of the heavens.

Mark 13:27 (King James Version)
27And then shall he send his angels, and shall gather together his elect from the four winds, from the uttermost part of the earth to the uttermost part of heaven.

This is why you must be prepared for the return of Jesus. God's vengeance will come upon those who are not prepared for Jesus return, or for those people who have not been living a Christian life.

Romans 12:19 (King James Version)
19Dearly beloved, avenge not yourselves, but rather give place unto wrath: for it is written, Vengeance is mine; I will repay, saith the Lord.

As a Christian believer you do not have to worry about getting vengeance towards those who have treated you wrong. God does not need for you repay others who have wrongfully harmed you in anyway. God's promises to repay them.

1 Thessalonians 4:17 (King James Version)
17Then we, which are alive and remain shall be caught up together with them in the clouds, to meet the Lord in the air: and so shall we ever be with the Lord.

This is part of the eternal life that we will have with Christ, so that we may live forever with Christ. Jesus is coming for you because he loves you. You may not believe that Jesus is coming for you, but he is.

Matthew 24:36 (King James Version)
36But of that day and hour Chynoweth no man, no, not the angels of heaven, but my Father only.

Only God knows the exact time he will return with his only son. It's all apart of the plan that God has in store for us. God loves you more than you can imagine. He love for you runs deep.

Revelation 22:14 (King James Version)
14Blessed are they that do his commandments that they may have right to the tree of life, and may enter in through the gates into the city.

We are to keep the commandments of God throughout life. Living according to his principals and commandments allows you to live a good life. Those who live a good life will enter the kingdom of heaven and have eternal life. This is your ultimate goal.

Jesus will come for those who choose to live a Christian life. Those who choose to honor God and his commandments.

John 6:38 (King James Version)
38For I came down from heaven, not to do mine own will, but the will of him that sent me.

John 6:39 (King James Version)
39And this is the Father's will which hath sent me, that of all which he hath given me I should lose nothing, but should raise it up again at the last day.

John 6:40 (King James Version)
40And this is the will of him that sent me, that every one, which seethe the Son, and believeth on him, may have everlasting life: and I will raise him up at the last day.

This is a promise from God that you will have ever lasting life for believing in Christ. Christ does not force you to believe in him. God only ask that you use your freewill choice to the best of your ability. We know that God's love for us runs deep. This is why he sent his only son to surrender his life for the life of others. This is why he will send his son to return so that we may have eternal life in the kingdom of heaven. God loves you more than you can imagine. More than you can dream of. God's love for us is shown throughout the bible through promises that he promises to complete through us as we complete our mission in life in which we have been placed in the world.

You must guard your heart, mind, body, soul, and spirit from the adversaries of the world. These spirits come to kill, steal, and destroy.

John 10:10 (King James Version)
10The thief cometh not, but for to steal, and to kill, and to destroy: I am come that they might have life, and that they might have it more abundantly.

The adversary knows that God has great things in store for you, which is why he works so hard to keep you away from the promises that God has in store for you. As the adversary attacks you that allows you to know that you are closet to your victory. The adversary wouldn't attack you so hard if he didn't know God has great things in store for you. This is why you must keep your head in the word of God. Remember your mission in life. We know that our mission in life is to save lives. We save life's with Romans 10:9, John 3:16, and John 6:40. These scriptures allow you to believe that Jesus died for you, so that you may be free from sin and have life eternal. God is a good God.

SUFFIX

The book, "The Price He Paid" is written so that you will be set free! So that you will be saved! So that you will enter the kingdom of heaven having eternal life!

It hurts me to my heart to have to witness anyone or any living soul have to witness damnation unto God in which you spend the remainder of your life in the kingdom of hell with the adversary.

I pray that through this book you to are saved.

Romans 10:9 teaches us that we too can be saved into the body of Christ. Romans 10:9 stats:

Romans 10:9
King James Version (KJV)
9That if thou shalt confess with thy mouth the Lord Jesus, and shalt believe in thine heart that God hath raised him from the dead, thou shalt be saved.

We know that Jesus died for our sins. Jesus blood was shed on the cross for our sins. Jesus died so that we will have eternal life in the kingdom of heaven!

John 3:16
King James Version (KJV)
16For God so loved the world that he gave his only begotten Son, that whosoever believeth in him should not perish, but have everlasting life.

I pray that through this journey you have found yourself. You have found the reason that God has created you. You have found the reason that God has given you life.

We all have wondered what the reason in which we have been created for. That is a testimony that is between you and God. Only God knows the answers to that question.

I pray that through a relationship that you build with God that God will show you the way that leads to life eternal. Show you the way that will manifest your life into a holy one.

You have been called out before the foundation of the world.

Ephesians 1:4
King James Version (KJV)
4According as he hath chosen us in him before the foundation of the world, that we should be holy and without blame before him in love:

Both Jesus and God loves you. God called you out before the foundation of the world to complete a mission in you. To complete a purpose for you.

Too many people in the world are living their life for others and for the world instead of God. We were put in this world temporarily for a purpose. For a mission. To complete a mission in Christ.

If we are going to live for God we are going to have to stop living our lives to the world standards and start living our lives for God. Remember we are not of this world.

John 15:19
King James Version (KJV)
19If ye were of the world, the world would love his own: but because ye are not of the world, but I have chosen you out of the world, therefore the world hatter you.

We are simply created or put in this world temporarily for mission to complete a mission through Christ.

Our mission in life is to save all souls so that we may all enter the kingdom of heaven. That's our mission in life. To save souls over that have not been saved. To save souls that have not yet been saved and have not yet entered the kingdom of God. God wants to see all of his creations enter the kingdom of heaven.

I pray that through this book, through the bible, through churches, through Christian television shows, and ministry that we can save all souls so that we all may enter the kingdom of heaven. I lift this up to God in the name of your son Jesus Christ Amen.

TRINITY

The Trinity consists of The Father, Son, and Holy Spirit.

A covenant with God, Christ, and self is made unto the Lord. The covenant in which you form cannot be broken. The Trinity is part of an incorruptible seed that cannot be broken.

The Trinity, The Father, Son, and Holy Ghost is set for Christians to believe the power that God has made known for Christian believers to believe in. The Father, Son, and Holy Ghost is made to establish Christian doctrine for a believer or believers faith to be made known.

Christians from the beginning of time have believed in The Trinity, its believers, ethics, morals, and standards. Through "The Trinity" we are made whole with Christ. The Trinity allows us to know that Jesus is the Son of God in which God created a seed in Mary for her to give birth to the Son of God.

We celebrate the birth of Jesus as we pray this prayer in the name of your son Jesus Christ Amen.

BAPTISM OF THE SPIRIT

This is a powerful book that talks about the power of the baptism of the spirit.

We all have a powerful testimony to share with others. We all have a powerful story to share with others. Some more powerful than others, but none greater than the next or greater than another.

This book is filled with pages, words, titles, chapters, and scriptures jammed packed with the fruit of the spirit for powerful healing power meant to heal the soul. This powerful testimony has been set on high for all Christian believers to witness and testify the goodness of God powerful testimony for any believers to become born again.

The baptism of the spirit is a holy covenant sacrifice that is made or formed with God.

The spirit of the water restores, replenishes, and refurbishes life! It cleanses the soul and cleanses life. The baptism of the spirit wipes away all sin, burden, strive, un-believe, pit falls, storms, and battles you may be facing.

The Baptism of the Spirit allows you to repent of your sins.

We repent of our sins so that we will be forgiven for the sins in which we commit. It cleanses you. It allows you to know that you have been saved, set free, restored, cleanses, replenished, and bought with a price into the kingdom of God. You are made holy. You are set free. You are set on high. You are made pure.

The Baptism of the Spirit is a holy temple of God. The temple is called and set from above. Set from above from the heavens. It's part of the kingdom of God. It's part of the plan that God has in store for you.

When you are baptized you are saved from the world. You are set free from the world. You are brought into the kingdom of God with the price that Jesus has paid for your soul.

The baptism of the spirit is part of a holy sanctuary. The Holy Spirit. The trinity. Father, son, and Holy Spirit. Both Jesus, God, and the Holy Spirit.

Through sacrifice, dedication, loyalty, commitment, freedom, and trust we are set free! We are saved, bought with a price. Free from sin, free from worry, free from harm, free from burden and free from strive.

It's part of the power name of your Lord and savior Jesus Christ. Through the baptism of the Holy Spirit you are not made whole in which you are saved. We lift this up to God in the name of your son Jesus Christ Amen.

REMEMBRANCE OF COMMUNION

The remembrance of communion is a sacrifice made holy unto God. The communion is made with God, for God, and by God.

Communion consist of increments of the holy sacrifice. The remembrance of the bread and wine for the price that Jesus paid on the cross for our sins.

Commitment to the body of Christ is required in the remembrance of communion.

The body of Christ is made whole through the remembrance of communion.

Through the remembrance of communion Jesus pays the price for one's sins.

Jesus died on the cross for our sins. Jesus blood was shed on the cross for our sins.

We partake in the bread in remembrance of the body, which was broken and crucified on the cross.

We partake in the wine to remember the blood that was shed on the cross for our sins so that we may be set free or may holy unto God.

I pray that through this prayer you are made holy. That you may be set free from all burden, strive, and un-belief. I pray that through the sacrifice of ones sins Jesus has paid the price for all sins. Through this prayer I pray that you are made whole. In the name of your son Jesus Christ Amen.

REPENTANCE OF SINS

The repentance of sins is made known unto man so that man may establish a covenant with God in the forgiveness of ones wrongs, mistakes, and sins.

God allows for man to come boldly to the throne of grace asking for forgiveness of ones mistakes in life.

Repentance of Sins is a powerful tool used to ask God forgiveness of ones mistakes in life.

We ask God forgiveness out of God's gentle grace and mercy so that we are forgiven for the mistakes that we have made in life.

Through repentance of sins you are able to come to God through prayer asking God for forgiveness for the mistakes one has made in life.

God knows that we often times fall short of the glory of God. God knows that we often times make mistakes in life. God understands and God forgives us. God forgives us for the mistakes that we have made in life. God forgives us for the wrongs that we have committed. God loves us un-conditionally which is why he sent his son Jesus to die on the cross for our sins so that that we are forgiven for the sins that or in which we commit.

We come to God asking him to forgive us for the sins that we have committed and God forgives us.

This method of forgiving is called repentance. We repent of our sins so that we will be forgiven. Forgiven for our sins, wrongs, and mistakes.

God understands that we all face pitfalls, storms, battles, burden, trials and tribulations which is why he sent his son Jesus on the cross for our sins.

This does not mean that we should take advantage of God sinning on purpose. We should approach the throne of God with humble hearts so that we will be forgiven for all that God has in store for us.

If we were not able to come to God for forgiveness we would live our lives in shame. We would live our lives with the burden of guilt in which destroys people, lives, the kingdom of God, and ultimately ourselves.

God forgives you for the sins in which you have committed. He loves you deeply. Remember God has formed an in-corruptible seed with us that cannot be broken. A covenant that cannot be destroyed. God loves you more than you can imagine which is why he sent his son Jesus to die on the cross for your sins.

We have a lot to be thankful for. Thank God everyday for the blessings that he has obtained upon you. God loves you much. God is a good God. In the name of your son Jesus Christ Amen.

Printed in the United States
By Bookmasters